KT-438-293

Allotments

Jane Eastoe

Allotments

*Inspiration and practical advice
for would-be smallholders*

 THE NATIONAL TRUST

First published in the United Kingdom in 2009 by
National Trust Books
10 Southcombe Street,
London W14 0RA

An imprint of Anova Books Company Ltd

ISBN 9781905400768

A CIP catalogue for this book is available from the British Library.

15 14 13 12 10 09
10 9 8 7 6 5 4 3 2

Repro by Mission Productions Ltd, Hong Kong.
Printed and bound by WS Bookwell Oy, Finland.

This book can be ordered direct from the publisher at the website
www.anovabooks.com, or try your local bookshop. Also available at
National Trust shops.

CONTENTS

INTRODUCTION

Fresh and delicious organic fruit and vegetables, plus armfuls of cut flowers, are the best advertisement for running your own allotment. Nothing beats the self-satisfied glow that comes from growing your own food and cooking it for family and friends. As television cook and organic campaigner Hugh Fearnley-Whittingstall puts it: 'I have not the least doubt that I am a better cook and a happier person for having absorbed the rhythm of the growing year.'

The fantastic thing about allotments is that they enable us to realise this Good Life fantasy. Gardens are generally too small for anything other than a small nod to fruit and veg cultivation, whereas an allotment, theoretically at least, is designed to allow you to grow sufficient produce to feed your family for a year.

Running an allotment in this day and age is unlikely to be the only thing standing between your family and starvation; however, the cost savings are considerable. Seasoned allotment holders try not to buy vegetables as a point of principle, so, aside from their annual allotment rental and the cost of seeds or plants, there is no outlay. Rising food prices, allied to global food shortages and the guilt of food miles, all combine to make the allotment package more attractive.

COMMUNITY SPIRIT

An allotment also has benefits beyond food production; these plots of land are home to intensely supportive and friendly communities. People will proffer advice, hand over seeds, divide plants, help you dig, entertain your children, throw a barbecue and give away their greens. While there may be a small element of competition – who has grown the biggest pumpkins, the tallest sunflowers or the straightest carrots – this is an egalitarian community where designer labels have no place and where old-fashioned values of ingenuity, sharing and creative make-do-and-mend are celebrated instead. At best allotments are physical demonstrations of sustainable living, forging a new role within the community that involves all generations, from schoolchildren to pensioners. Allotments today are also green corridors that provide shelter for wildlife.

The physical benefits are huge; gardening on this scale will help to keep you fit as well as providing a balm for the soul. Weight-loss aside, stress, tension, anger and frustration can all be eased with a little double digging and there is nothing more soothing than the quiet and gentle activity of picking your own beans, peas, raspberries and asparagus. How can things not feel a little better when life is taken back to basics in this very real way?

Children relish allotment life and what better environment for them to start to learn gardening? You would be advised to keep some toys there and perhaps make a little space for a sand pit with a lid – the space needs to be fun for them if they are to let you get on with your work. Please remember that allotments can be dangerous places for small children – other gardeners may well leave pieces of broken glass propped up for use as required, chemicals or secateurs may not always be put away and water butts are terribly inviting if you are small.

The practical need for man to till the soil is part of our common history – we have always required small areas of land for food production – and for centuries there has been an ongoing struggle between those who control the land and those who are desperate to use it. The Saxons were able to clear land and hold it for common usage, but after the Norman conquests, land ownership was chiefly in the hands of the crown, the nobility and the church. With various enclosure acts, problems became more acute. The first mention of 'allotted' land comes from late in the reign of Elizabeth I when allotments of land were attached to tenant cottages in recompense for the repossession of common land.

In 1649 one Gerrard Winstanley led a group of hungry men in protest that the common people of England had been robbed of their birthrights by the Normans. They took over common land in St George's Hill, Surrey in a mass protest and became known as 'Diggers'. With food prices at an all-time high, they began, scandalously, to cultivate it. Winstanley claimed that all men had a 'right to dig'. He argued that if the common people of England would form themselves into self-supporting communes there would be no place in society for the ruling classes; all men, he said, were equal. The movement spread and although the growing of peas and beans seems mild enough, the Diggers were subdued. Nevertheless, the basic 'right to dig' concept still holds true today.

In the Industrial Revolution thousands abandoned the subsistence way of life and relocated to the cities to work in factories, but many were facing starvation and had no land on which to grow their own food. The General Enclosure Act of 1845 recognised that provision should be made for the landless poor in the form of field gardens – these were to be limited in size to ¼ acre (0.1 hectare). In reality there was little land made available, and even that was largely confined to rural areas. Nonetheless, the act marks the start of the Allotment Movement.

THE FIRST ALLOTMENTS

In 1887 the Allotments and Cottage Gardens Compensation for Crops Act forced local authorities to provide land for allotments if there was a demand for them. The Small Holding and Allotments Act of 1908 further imposed responsibilities on the parish and local councils to provide land if required, a principle that still holds true today. Significantly, the Victorians introduced a small levy to be charged annually to allotment holders, to avoid the stigma that such land was only for the poor. The popular view was that allotments were to be encouraged: not only did they prevent starvation, they kept people busy and out of the ale house.

Food shortages during World War One saw the demand for allotments increase. Councils were finally forced to make proper land provision where none previously existed. The railway companies, who held small pockets of wasteland along their tracksides, allotted this to railway workers so that it could be put to productive use. Many still remain, a legacy of those years, when the number of working plots increased from 600,000 to 1,500,000. After the Great War the demand for allotments fell and parcels of land were clawed back and used for housing.

The pattern was to be repeated in World War Two when German blockades effectively hit food imports – it was quickly apparent that food shortages would become acute. The Dig for Victory campaign encouraged everyone to turn over their gardens to food production, no matter how small, and allotments were fully utilised – even public parks were used to grow food. The nation rose to the challenge and it has been estimated that some 1.4 million allotments produced 1.3 million tonnes of produce – one fifth of the nation's food. Nella Last took part in the Mass Observation project (social research set up to study everyday life) and her diary entry for Sunday, 16 March, 1941 highlights the change of attitude:

> *'After tea, my husband said, "I'm going to do a bit of gardening – I've an onion bed to make." He spoke so importantly that I chuckled to myself. He is planning and talking of what he will plant – so much better than when I had to coax and bully him to get a few cabbages.'*

Demand for land after the war resulted in The Allotment Act of 1950, which recommended a provision of 4 acres (1.6 hectares) of land per one thousand head of population. Food rationing continued until 1954, which ensured that allotments were still a valued resource. But after this time there was a decline in interest: sampling the good life meant putting your feet up and enjoying a shop-bought TV dinner. Principles that made a virtue out of growing your own fruits and vegetables seemed dull and old fashioned.

It is very hard to find definitive statistics for the numbers of plots in use today: estimates indicate that there are some 330,000 plots across the country and demand has rocketed since the mid-1990s. Theoretically, if councils take allotment land away they have to make suitable provision elsewhere, the Manor Garden Allotments in Hackney Wick, East London being a case in point. Their 4.5 acres (1.8 hectares) of land, donated by a philanthropist back in 1900, has been utilised as part of the 2012 Olympic site; however, protests have ensured that not only has a new site been provided in the interim, but that the land will be reinstated after the Olympics.

The Allotment Movement is going strong and in the inner cities there are long waiting lists for a plot. Sales of vegetable seeds are outstripping those of flowers, by an impressive 60 per cent year on year in spring 2008. What's more, the social make-up of the allotment is changing: women are challenging these bastions of male dominance. In the 1980s just 3 per cent of allotment holders were women; today the figure is closer to 20 per cent and rising. Age profiles are changing too; allotment holders are getting younger, with some 35 per cent being under 50.

There is genuine concern about food quality; we want to know where our food has come from, as well as what it has been fed on, grown in and sprayed with. The perfect solution is to take control and grow your own – and where better than the allotment? This is your space, to do with as you will, to grow what you please, how you please and when you please – your own domain and a tiny slice of paradise!

HOW TO GET AN
ALLOTMENT

The bliss of owning an allotment is that your location,
theoretically at least, is no deterrent. Wherever you live,
city, town or country, there should be an allotment near you,
though you may well have to put your name on a waiting
list. In many areas of the country the wait may not be as
long as you think; most people can expect to get an
allotment in around a year, some in far less time.

There are still plenty of sites across the country where
allotment plots are sitting empty and neglected. Inner
London and some of the largest cities are the exceptions and
waiting lists there can be off-putting. Councils tend to deal
with evictions and vacancies on an annual basis at the year
end, so plots often become available in early spring. Don't be
deterred by a long waiting list: get your name down. As much
as anything else, this will make councils aware of the existing
demand: they are obligated to provide a sufficient number of
allotments. In practice this equation is hard to manage. With
take-up rates fluctuating wildly across the decades, councils
have been inclined to sell off unused land and then have no
fall back when demand increases. The question remains, just
what is a sufficient number of allotments in ratio to demand?
The only solution is to keep the pressure up and, when you
finally acquire an allotment, make a commitment to put in
the time to maintain it – your efforts will be repaid tenfold.

Most allotments are owned and managed by local authorities.
They can be statutory sites, which are protected by law, or

temporary sites, which are rented on a pro-tem basis. Some sites are privately owned; the most beautiful one I have ever seen was behind a 14th-century church. The easiest way to find out who owns a parcel of allotments is to ask an existing tenant – they will be happy to give you the low down and can often let you know if any plots are vacant or whether or not there is a waiting list.

RULES AND REGULATIONS

Plots are rented on a tenancy basis for a year – the costs vary from around £20 to £80 per annum – and in return you will be supplied with a key and, hopefully, access to a tap – vital for tea making, if nothing else. You will also be issued with a set of rules and regulations. These vary from site to site, but are in the most part good common sense. There may be restrictions on planting trees, using hosepipes, lighting bonfires or keeping livestock.

The last point can be fought. Legislation entitles plot holders to keep hens and rabbits providing it is not for trade or business. I am a great chicken enthusiast. A couple of hens will usefully work over an overgrown allotment, or rake over and fertilise a section of cleared ground. They are not noisy, as long as there is no cockerel, and they are both an enthusiastic work force and a boon to the compost heap – plus they provide the best eggs you will have ever tasted pretty much on a daily basis! Your only commitment is to get to the allotment both morning and evening for feeding, watering and housing – though if a few of you get together this can be done on a rota. Livestock must not present a health hazard, or be a nuisance. For advice on current health legislation and chicken keeping contact the Department for Environment, Food and Rural Affairs (Defra). Beehives also sit naturally in the allotment environment – bees are vital for the fertilisation of flowers, as well as a source of your own honey.

Allotment holders are duty bound to keep their plots cultivated; many allotments are given up because people have not been able to find enough time to maintain them. It is not fair on your neighbours to allow weeds to take hold. The very minimum you should expect to spend there is approximately four hours a week, though this will really only enable you to just about keep control. Eight hours a week will allow you to develop a really good allotment. Remember that there are seasonal fluctuations in workloads; expect to do rather more in the summer than you do in the winter.

HOW BIG IS A PLOT?

The size of an allotment is variable. The ancient measurements of rods are used; most plots measure 10 square rods – around 250m^2 (300yd^2). Increasingly councils are happy to divide plots into halves or quarters, or indeed for them to be shared. There is an argument against splitting plots, as the original idea behind an allotment was that a full-sized measurement enables you to feed your family for the year. However many women find a full-sized plot daunting and, speaking personally – with two young children in tow – I couldn't have managed anything larger than a half-sized plot.

Many allotment holders form local associations, which can have advantages – manure or materials can be bought in bulk and discounts negotiated with nurseries and seed suppliers.

GETTING STARTED

A well-planned allotment can produce an impressive amount of food. Production records taken from carefully tended individual plots over the years remain constant: if you put in the energy, your 250m² (300yd²) plot is capable of producing three quarters of a ton of food annually – you would need to spend around £1,500 to buy that amount of produce.

Pests and diseases aside, if you are getting it right on your allotment you are very likely to produce more food than you can eat. A fruit and vegetable plot is very seductive – it tempts you to grow just a few more plants, to try another new variety, or to utilise every last millimetre of space. Betty MacDonald, in her autobiographical story *The Egg and I*, highlights the excess:

> 'Bob made garden rows as straight as dies, spaced to the inch, and his seeds came up the correct distance from one another. When he planted a seed it immediately got busy and sprouted and appeared in exactly the allotted time... In rows about fifty feet long, stretching from the sweet peas to the rhubarb and herbs, were peas, early and late, carrots, turnips, beets, cauliflower, Swiss chard, sweet corn, parsnips, beans, cucumbers, tomatoes, squash, radishes... Bob made an asparagus bed, which I estimated when in full production, would take care of that portion of the United States extending from the Columbia River to the Pacific Ocean.'

When tackling a plot for the first time, don't overstretch yourself. Many newcomers tackle too much to begin with and are overwhelmed by the whole allotment experience; they can't keep pace with the harvesting of their crops let alone the relentless weeding. Take a little time to get to know your plot and those of your neighbours. Work out what kind of soil you have, check on the aspect of your plot, establish where the sun rises and sets, see how the land lies and take note of problem areas that are shady, dry or boggy. Find out what varieties of which plants grow easily in your particular soil. Finally, unless you have the strength and determination of Superman, don't try to clear an overgrown plot in one season – cover up chunks of it with old carpets and let nature do the work for you. Plan out what you want to grow and how you want your allotment to function, and work towards the end result little by little.

START WITH THE SOIL

Dan Pearson, garden designer and all-round plant expert, quotes an old saying 'a pound on the hole and a penny on the plant' to emphasise the importance of the growing medium. If you get the soil right, you can make all sorts of other mistakes and the plant will forgive you. Get it wrong and plants will struggle to survive and fall prey to every pest and disease going. Healthy plant growth depends on soil quality; plants do not thrive on a starvation diet any better than we do.

MAKING COMPOST

Good soil is rich in decomposing organic matter that is teeming with micro-organisms and insects. Compost is the perfect medium for improving soil. It's free and it's eco-friendly; it's recycling at its best, with household waste and green garden rubbish being transformed into nutrient-rich plant food. A pile of rubbish left in the corner of the allotment will not produce compost; the conditions must be right for this miracle to occur. Composting speeds up the natural process of decomposition due to the higher temperatures generated in a good compost heap, which can reach 60°C (140°F) in summer and will steam on a cold winter morning. Heat is generated by the exothermic action of bacteria as they decompose the organic matter.

A good compost bin is paramount; the larger the bin the more heat it will generate and the faster you will produce compost. As a basic rule it should be 1m² (1yd²) in area, well-ventilated, with good circulation and drainage, and an effective cover to keep rain out. See colour section for illustration.

WHAT TO ADD

Garden clippings and household waste are principal ingredients, but all sorts of bits and pieces can go in: shredded twigs, chopped-up newspaper, coffee grounds – the broadest definition is anything that has ever lived. There must be a good mix of ingredients – huge dollops of grass clippings will just slow down the process and large branches will take years to rot. A general rule is to aim for two-thirds brown waste to one-third green. The brown is the carbon found in fibrous material such as stems, twigs, roots, straw, cardboard and old woollen or cotton clothes; the green is the nitrogen found in grass, plant leaves, stems, weeds and flowers. The brown components rot down more slowly, but they add structure and create air pockets, which aids air circulation. The composting process relies on a mix of aerobic and anaerobic bacteria growing on the waste and breaking it down into soil – without the air circulation the anaerobic bacteria dominate, slowing the rate of decomposition and making the heap smelly. Once a fortnight add an activator to help speed up the process – chicken manure or urine are ideal (male composters have a natural advantage here).

The compost should be forked over once a month until it is 'cooked', a process that can take three to six months depending on the time of year and the basic mix. Don't put perennial weeds into the compost as they will survive and grow – sling them into a covered bucket with water and when they have decomposed to a vile-smelling slime, toss that on the compost. Never put anything in the compost that will attract vermin, such as meat or fish waste.

OTHER SOIL IMPROVERS

Leaf mould, which as its name suggests is formed of rotting fallen leaves, is less rich in nutrients but bulks up compost and makes it go further. Rake up leaves, put them in black bags, leave for a year and bingo! For the best results, ensure the leaves are damp rather than dry and fork a few ventilation holes into the fabric of the black bag so that the leafmould compost can breathe, rather than go to an anaerobic mess.

Manure from horses, cows, pigs and chickens must be well rotted before it is incorporated into the soil. If you want to garden organically remember that manure, although it comes from the most natural of sources, is not necessarily organic – check your source if this is important to you.

Green manure or compost is a crop that is specifically grown to be incorporated into the soil. Plants such as the green manure lupin (*Lupinus angustifolius*), winter tares (*Vicia sativa* spp.), buckwheat (*Fagopyrum esculentum*) and the poached egg plant (*Limnanthes douglasii*) will all add nutrients and organic matter. The crop is generally killed off by frost, then hoed or dug in.

SOIL TYPES

Soil texture is graded according to its clay, silt and sand content; the size and proportion of these particles affects the behaviour of the soil. A loam soil has the perfect mix of mineral particle sizes with a 40-40-20 (sand-silt-clay) concentration. This mix offers high fertility with good drainage and water retention. All soils can be improved with a combination of compost, manure and lime, as required.

Clay soil is a heavy, slow-draining soil, often with a high nutrient content. It is slow to warm up in spring and the soil structure is easily damaged by compaction. Sandy soil is light and free-draining, easy to work but lacking in fertility. It warms up quickly in spring and can be improved by adding organic matter, fertiliser and frequent irrigation. Chalk soil is moderately fertile, but also shallow, stony and free-draining. It too warms up quickly in spring. Silt is more moisture retentive and fertile than sandy soil. It warms up quickly in spring but its structure is easily damaged by compaction.

ADDING FERTILISER

Fruit and vegetables are hungry plants and they will make heavy demands on your nutrient-rich soil. Extra feeds may be required in the form of fertiliser. These are rated according to their nitrogen (N), phosphorous (P) and potassium (K) content. Nitrogen stimulates growth and leaves, phosphorous benefits the roots and potassium boosts fruiting and overall disease resistance.

If you prefer a more natural alternative to packaged fertilisers you can buy pelleted chicken manure or make your own nutritious liquid manures from comfrey (*Symphytum officinale*) or stinging nettles (*Urtica dioica*). Comfrey is known as a dynamic accumulator because it absorbs nutrients from deep in the soil and carries them up to its leaves – it is a valuable plant to have on the allotment. To make comfrey fertiliser, take a large bucket with a lid, put in as many comfrey leaves as will fit, weigh down with stones, cover and leave for five to six weeks then draw off the brown syrupy liquid that has accrued. It will smell vile, but is terribly good for your plants. The mix produces a high potassium feed that will need to be diluted 15:1 before use. After straining your mix, throw the sodden leaves on the compost heap.

Nettle fertiliser can be made using the same method, but tear the leaves and stems first – wear gloves for this – before adding water to the mix. The resulting liquid, a rich nitrogen fertiliser, is ready for use after four weeks and needs to be diluted 10:1.

It is possible to overdo the fertiliser, resulting in lush, sappy growth and poor fruiting. The secret to success is getting the soil in good condition before you begin, then giving extra feeds judiciously and only where specified.

Weed are just plants in the wrong place, but they will compete with your precious crops for light, nutrition, space and water and should be removed. Digging and hoeing are the most effective mechanisms: if you want to garden organically you can't use chemical controls. Try to remove every piece of weed root when you are weeding as even the tiniest pieces of some species can sprout new plants. The worst offenders are couch grass (*Elymus repens*), bindweed (*Calystegia sepium*) and ground elder (*Aegopodium podagraria*). Stinging nettles (*Urtica dioica*), whose presence indicates good, nitrogen-rich soil, attract many useful invertebrates – 27 species are wholly dependent on it. While it may never have any status as a companion plant, it does have wildlife value on the outskirts of your plot. If you dig nettles up, put them on the compost heap – they are packed with nitrogen.

Regular hoeing and weeding will stop this job becoming a real chore, but if you neglect your plot the weeds will inevitably take hold very quickly. As any allotment holder will tell you, if a plot is left untouched for six months – or less in spring and summer – it will become completely overgrown.

MULCHES

Mulches are a remarkably effective way of keeping weeds at bay once you have prepared a patch of ground – or you can use them to clear an area of weeds. A mulch is any material applied to the top of the soil that can smother weeds, condition the soil, keep weed seeds at bay and inhibit moisture loss. Old discarded carpet works very effectively

as does black plastic, but it will take a year or more to
thoroughly clear a patch of weeds. Avoid rubber-backed carpet
as it breaks up into the soil – carpet shops take up plenty of
old carpet and will generally be happy for you to take it off
their hands. You can buy porous plastic membrane that lets
water through but keeps weeds out, or you can use paper and
cardboard, but these will need to be weighted down with a
bark or cocoa-shell mulch on top. Compost and manure make
good conditioning surface mulches; they won't control weeds
but they will improve the quality of the soil. When you use a
mulch, as a general rule make a slight depression in it around
individual plants to encourage rainwater to run towards them.

GET GROWING

The fun part for the allotment holder is choosing which
varieties of vegetable to grow. It's a good idea to note what
flourishes on other plots – it is always best to work with the
site you have and not to fight against nature. When starting
out I would advocate a gentle approach: begin with the
simplest, most straightforward crops and those that the family
likes – and leave the likes of celery, okra, melons or grapes
until you are more experienced. Make a plan of what you
want to grow, work out which vegetables will need to form
part of a rotation system (see page 23) and plan your plot
accordingly. Record what you planted – and where – in
a notebook for future reference. Later in the season you
can note how the different varieties performed.

There is an amazing selection of seed to tempt growers; new
varieties of purple tomatoes, red carrots or orange beetroot
are fun to try, but and sheer range on offer is astounding.

Allotment holders Peter and Ann Sutherland, who ran a greengrocers shop in Wye, Kent have seen the market transformed: 'In the 1980s we used to celebrate the sale of a green pepper,' Peter says, 'there is so much more variety on the market today.'

Plan to grow successive crops so that you have a regular supply of fresh seasonal vegetables. It is eating your produce so very fresh that brings the taste benefits. 'I used to buy my fruit in and keep it for a day or two until it was almost perfect to eat, then I would put it on display,' notes Peter Sutherland. 'My produce was very fresh, but at best it would have been at least a day old. Some of the produce you see in the large supermarkets looks half dead to me.' The secret is to grow successively and pick as required. 'Allotment produce is so tasty because it is just picked or dug. If you keep it in the fridge for a week you will have lost that advantage,' Ann says. These former greengrocers now live off their allotment entirely; the only vegetable they buy is carrots, which they have never had much success with.

PRACTISE ROTATION

Vegetable growers need to follow the principles of crop rotation. Vegetables fall into nine main family groups and closely related vegetables are susceptible to the same sets of problems. If you continue to grow the same vegetable, or its close relation, in the same spot you will build up associated pests and diseases in the soil. By growing vegetables in successive positions over a four-year cycle, these problems are generally avoided (more information can be found in the chapter on Vegetables, see pages 29–31).

MAKE A SEED BED

Reserve a space in your allotment for a seed bed where young crops can be protected and nurtured. This space will be a focus for your attention and it will give your plants the best start possible. A seed bed should be dug over, weeds and stones removed and garden compost or farmyard manure incorporated the autumn before you plan to use it. Turn the soil over and allow cold winter conditions to break down the hard clods (1). In late winter or early spring work the soil to reduce lumps; use the rake tines to comb the surface and the rake face to firm it and tamp it down (2). When conditions are dry tread, the soil to break it down further and rake again (3). Don't use the bed until you have allowed weed seeds to develop for a couple of weeks – remove these and you will have cleared the worst of the annual weeds in advance of planting – some people use flame guns but that seems a little overdramatic and raises all sorts of health and safety issues!

 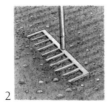 

WHAT ABOUT SPACING?

As something of a natural rebel, I have always found the rules associated with allotment planting a bit of a turn off. If, like me, the concept of pulling out a tape measure every time you plant a seed fills you with horror, then take heart. Allotment planting does not have to be completely rigid – certainly it is helpful to know how deeply a seed should be planted or how far apart rows of broad beans should be spaced, but the backs of seed packets give you this information. It doesn't matter if your rows are wobbly or your spacing is off, as long as your plants are thriving. That said, there is a perfect beauty to the well-ordered allotment that I shall probably never attain; the plants line up and stand to attention and there is a continuity to the sowing, planting, flowering, fruiting and cropping production line throughout the year. Seeds can be sown in wide drills, narrow drills or in situ. See colour section for illustration.

PESTS AND DISEASES

The sensible gardener will respect the rich diversity of wildlife in their allotment. An insect or animal only becomes a pest when it has an adverse effect on our plants and it is often perfectly possible to deal with it without resorting to chemicals. Chemical controls are not selective in what they kill: if you wipe out an aphid infestation with chemicals you will also lose ladybirds and hoverflies – their natural predators. With fewer predators in the garden the aphid problem will only become more acute the following year, taking possibly several years for a balance to be restored.

Some pests call for the use of barrier methods. Nets, meshes and fleeces can work wonders against birds, rabbits, carrot flies and cutworms. Slugs can be discouraged with crushed eggshells, wood ash or sand, and caterpillars can be picked off and disposed of on the compost heap. Orange halves, saucers of beer or milk will tempt slugs away from plants.

Straw-filled flowerpots are attractive to earwigs and jam jars filled with sugary liquid will attract wasps – cover the jars with paper, pierced to let them in but not out. Deter birds with fine cotton threads woven around plants or hang CDs on a string – see colour section for illustration. Change these regularly, though, as birds get used to them.

Organic gardeners can weigh the dice in their favour by making informed plant selections. Choose fruit and vegetable varieties that have good resistance to specific pests and diseases. Ensure that basic measures such as hygiene and crop rotation are adhered to. Hygiene is in essence simply keeping your plot in good order: clear up after weeding, promptly remove and burn diseased plants and leaves to stop the spread of infection, remove rotting fruit and veg, keep secateurs sharp so that pruning cuts are neat and clean, and always use clean compost to grow seeds to give them the best start in life. Methods of biological control can have an impact. Actively encourage natural predators into the allotment: hoverflies, ladybirds, lacewings and assorted beetles are all especially effective aphid and slug controllers. Put out nesting boxes, bat roosts and hedgehog dens; dig a pond to attract slug-hungry frogs and toads (although if your allotment is owned by a parish council or county council you should ensure they have insurance to cover pond accidents before you embark on any work). Hoverfly larvae consume far more aphids than ladybirds and the adults are attracted to yellow flowers; by planting yellow companion species close to any plants that suffer from regular aphid attacks, you are tempting a pest away from your valuable crop. If you attract the insects, the birds, bats and hedgehogs will follow, then you can relax and let nature take care of the problems for you.

Part of the beauty of an allotment is the ingenuity people use to create sheds, storage containers or allotment furniture; there is a refreshing waste-not-want-not approach that is an antidote to our disposable culture. Garden furniture can be cobbled together from almost anything and all sorts of bits and pieces can be uncovered in skips. Old wooden wine boxes, drawers or wholesale-size food tins all make wonderful containers for seeds or saladings – just drill some drainage holes in the bottom first. Drawers or old glazed kitchen cabinets can be used to make one-off cold frames.

Don't buy plastic plant pots – make your own from old newspapers. Fold a sheet of paper in half, roll it around a tube with the folded edge kept neat at the top. Pull the tube out and scrunch up the excess paper at the bottom, pushing it inside the tube to form a base – et voila!

One of the easiest ways to pick up a shed is to advertise for one. People are always removing old ones from their garden and are only too pleased to find a home for them.

Support woodland management – and ultimately sustainability and British wildlife – by using native alternatives to imported bamboo canes; look out for locally produced chestnut, hazel, birch and willow beanpoles and pea sticks.

All this hard work will make you thirsty. A Thermos is all very well but, better still, keep an old-fashioned kettle and camping-gas stove in your shed. This will make you very popular with your neighbours.

VEGETABLES

Growing vegetables is the very essence of allotment owning –
you may grow fruit or even cut flowers but in many people's
books that is just messing around. Vegetables are what count:
proper, grown-up, essential food that requires seed sowing,
double digging and crop rotation. Nothing else gives quite the
same feeling of satisfaction as a good crop of vegetables.
This is what providing for your family is all about:
producing fresh, tasty, pesticide-free, economical food. It's
back-to-nature, honest-to-goodness hard work that anyone
would be proud of. Never mind a personal trainer – burn up
a few calories and strengthen your muscles rotovating,
weeding and gathering in your crops.

Vegetables are demanding plants; they need an open,
sunny site, a good, rich soil and plenty of tender loving
care. Turn your back and that courgette flower will turn into a
giant marrow, while carrots and onions will suddenly bolt into
flower. Tender plants, such as sweetcorn, have to be started
unnaturally early in the season and mollycoddled through
spring if they are to fruit in our poor summers.

The vegetables you grow can be selected for flavour rather
than for yield, which is by necessity the commercial grower's
principal concern. To use your allotment effectively, exercise
some restraint in the planning and planting of your crops;
successive plantings will ensure that you end up with two
or three cabbages per week and not 30 all at once. It is this
quietly repetitive work, popping in a few seeds each week,
not planting the whole lot in one go, which will make your
plot productive – a glut of produce can end up being wasteful.

Crop rotation must also be taken into consideration or your vegetables will fall prey to all manner of pests and diseases. It may appear complex at first, but the theory is simple: by growing different families of crops in successive positions over a four-year calendar, a build-up of soil-borne pests and diseases can be avoided. Vegetables fall into nine major family groups and these can be divided into the three main rotation groups (see colour section for illustration), with the same requirements and fallibilities, as follows.

LEGUMES AND PODS – this includes broad beans, French beans, okra, peas and runner beans.

BRASSICAS – including broccoli, Brussels sprouts, cauliflower, cabbage, kohlrabi, kale, pak choi, radish, swede and turnip.

SOLANACEOUS, TUBEROUS AND ROOT CROPS – including aubergine, beetroot, carrot, celery, celeriac, parsnip, potato, sweet potato, sweet pepper and tomato.

It makes good sense to practise rotation, for although the basic idea is simple – leave it as long as possible before you grow potatoes or brassicas on the same spot – in fact there are other considerations, such as soil condition, to be taken into account.

Saladings, stem vegetables, the onion family and the pumpkin family can be fitted in as you like within the rotating crops, depending on space. Herbs are often best grown separately from vegetables as some experts consider that aromatic perennials inhibit the germination of vegetable seeds.

A plan is all that is required – just make sure you keep your notebook somewhere safe so that in each successive year you know where to plant your vegetable groups. It is also a good idea to record how your crops performed so that you can assess different varieties in terms of vigour, time management and – perhaps most importantly – taste.

On a final note, growing vegetables is often seen as a man's work, as Monty Don explains in his book *The Prickotty Bush*:

> *'I was brought up with an unspoken belief that the vegetable garden was the macho end of horticulture, the part where a man could do what a man must do. This did not, with hindsight, mean that my mother and sisters were not allowed to weed or work long hours picking sprouts on a raw January day, but it remained a male province. Perhaps this was because it was the one part of the garden where there was regular heavy digging and this was done by men. Consequently the rows were kept straight and long and the three main plots a proper sort of rectangular shape. None of your nancy-boy potagers in our garden thank you very much.'*

While I would hate to suggest that growing vegetables is man's work, I do think that some women can be daunted by trying to tackle too much in the way of macho vegetable growing in their early days of allotment holding. Women, and men with bad backs, should bear in mind that there are plenty of vegetables that do not demand regular double digging and it is at least possible to make your allotment successfully productive with less back-breaking crops such as saladings and soft fruit, or perennial crops such as asparagus and artichokes to begin with. As you get fitter and stronger, the likes of potatoes and cauliflowers can be tackled.

SALADINGS

Saladings appreciate a good, rich soil for rapid growth so, when preparing a salad bed, dig in plenty of manure. They are perfect for planting among other vegetables as they are fast growing and small. Most of them are easy to grow, can be sown *in situ* (always a boon), keep on cropping throughout the year and can be eaten raw. What more could you ask?

AMERICAN LAND CRESS (*Barbarea verna*)

This peppery plant is a good alternative to watercress and can be grown in the shade in moist soil. It will need watering in dry weather or the leaves can become very tough. Sow the seeds *in situ* and make successive sowings throughout the summer, thinning plants to 15cm (6in) intervals. Plants should keep producing leaves until winter.

CHICORY (*Cichorium intybus*) AND ENDIVE (*Cichorium endivia*)

Chicory and endive are close relations and it is quite easy to get the two plants confused: both have bitter leaves and both can be forced. The great cookery writer Arabella Boxer has admitted:

> *'Like many other English people, I live in a permanent state of confusion between chicory and endives.'*

A state that is not helped by the French and Americans, who regularly call chicory endive and endive chicory. A very loose definition is that endive is eaten much like lettuce while chicory takes around nine months to grow and is forced, but there are exceptions in both plants. As far as I am concerned you need to be very dedicated to want to go through the palaver of growing these plants for forcing.

For endive sow the seeds *in situ* and thin to a distance of 30cm (12in). Choose between Frisée, which is planted in early summer and forms lush green foliage like a lettuce, and the tighter, broad-leaved, upright plants known as Batavian (or Escarole). These should be planted late in summer, though the leaves will need to be covered with a cloche to protect them from frost. If they are too bitter for your taste – these plants are related to the dandelion after all – then you can follow tradition and blanch them by tying the leaves together and covering them with a bucket for two weeks before harvesting.

Belgian chicory is grown for forcing. Sow seeds in summer, lift the plants at around four months of age, trim the roots and leaves, then place the remaining plant in a bucket for forcing. Pack the bucket with sand or sandy soil and bring it into the house for warmth. Keep plants watered and the bucket covered, and the tight, pale leaves – the chicons – will be ready for eating in around three weeks. Radicchio, the wonderful red-leafed chicory, can be sown *in situ* in early summer and can be eaten without forcing and cut repeatedly.

LAMB'S LETTUCE *(Valerianella locusta)*

Lamb's lettuce commonly features in ready-packaged salad mixes, but many people don't think to grow it themselves. It has a delicious tangy flavour and is very good, lightly steamed though it should be well washed for it always seems to be earthy. It contains three times as much vitamin C as lettuce. It grows wild in Europe and seeds readily; sow *in situ* and thin plants to 20cm (8in) when they have three leaves. Sow a fresh batch every fortnight; it will keep going until quite late in the year. The leaves don't last long when picked; pop them in a plastic bag and store in the refrigerator for a couple of days only.

LETTUCE *(Lactuca sativa)*

Neat and tidy lines of lettuce should feature in every allotment. They are quite easy to grow, though they need regular watering to keep the leaves crisp and succulent, and to stop them bolting. There are many varieties, from Lollo Rossa to Iceberg and Cos – grow a selection to keep your salads interesting. Many varieties can be grown *in situ*, but early and late varieties will need to be started out under glass. Lettuce doesn't like high temperatures, so avoid sowing seed in the height of summer. Thin the seedlings to 15–30cm (6–12in) intervals depending on the variety. Make successive sowings every fortnight to ensure a continual crop. Slugs love lettuce and aphids can be a problem; use a companion plant to try to attract aphids elsewhere and use biological controls to keep slugs at bay. Solutions containing millions of microscopic nematodes – killer parasites – are an effective biological control; these can be used between March and October and are readily available from suppliers of biological controls.

ROCKET *(Eruca sativa)*

Rocket is blissfully easy to grow and the peppery leaves are fabulous in salads and mixed with pasta. Sow the seeds *in situ* at four-weekly intervals for a continuous supply, thinning them to 15cm (6in). Rocket needs watering in summer and does best planted in the shade. Pick off leaves or cut whole plants, which should resprout.

SPINACH *(Spinacia oleracea)*

Spinach is a valuable allotment plant. It can give you leaves almost throughout the year if you keep sowing seeds every few weeks, though it will need protection from frosts in autumn. Summer and winter varieties are available. The young leaves are delicious raw, steamed or fried in butter. Spinach will grow happily in the shade of taller plants. It enjoys a rich moisture-retentive soil and one that is neutral to alkaline. As with chard (see below), the seeds do better if they are soaked overnight prior to planting. Sow straight into the ground, spaced at 10cm (4in) intervals. If your allotment is dry, spinach may bolt – it does need moisture.

SWISS CHARD *(Beta vulgaris,* subsp. *cicla,* var. *flavescens)*

Chard is one of my favourite vegetables. It looks wonderful, both when growing and cooked on the plate – a symphony of glorious colour with red, purple, pink, orange and yellow stems and midribs. Ruby chard has fabulous red roots (which doesn't count for anything, but secretly pleases me very much indeed); perhaps this should be expected for it is a relative of the beetroot. The leaves can be eaten raw, popped into stir fries, sautéed or steamed like spinach; the taste is faintly bitter, but cooking removes much of this flavour if it is not to your taste. Young leaves are the tenderest and can be picked throughout the growing season. Some people cut the stems out first and cook them separately, but I like the contrast in textures. Seeds can be sown in spring and late summer and the plant will often continue producing leaves into winter. Soak seeds overnight before planting in seed trays under cover. Space plants at 30cm (12in) intervals in sun or partial shade. The plant originates from the seaside and appreciates seaweed fertilisers.

STEM VEGETABLES

Growing celery is a serious business and if you don't have loads of time on your hands it probably isn't worth the trouble. Celeriac, on the other hand, is far less temperamental. Although it is technically a root vegetable, I'm including it here because you can use the shoots instead of celery in casseroles and soups. The root will carry on maturing and then you have the bonus of using that too!

CELERIAC *(Apium graveolens* var. *rapaceum)*

The stems of celeriac can be used in much the same way as celery, but celeriac has the advantage of being much hardier and easier to grow. It can stay in the ground right through winter if given the protection of a cloche or straw. Sow the seeds in mid to late spring and keep under cover; harden off seedlings outside when all danger of frost has passed and then plant out, spacing them at 30cm (12in) intervals. Keep well watered and give a liquid feed every fortnight. Keep snipping off and using the shoots – apart from providing delicious greens it helps the root to mature. To use the crown, cut off the roots and the grubby exterior – then cut up the creamy flesh and use it as you please – it is delicious boiled then mashed with butter and cream. You can even try cooking celeriac chips: the chips are best blanched in boiling water for a few minutes before frying. The good news is celeriac has less starch than most root vegetables so it contains fewer calories.

CARDOON (*Cynara cardunculus*)

Cardoons are believed to be an early ancestor of the globe artichoke, but the plant is grown annually not for its flower head, but for its leaves and stems. Sow seeds in April in manure-rich trenches, spaced at 60cm (2ft) intervals; keep them under cloches for their first month. They need plenty of water and a weekly feed of liquid fertiliser over the summer. When plants have finished growing in mid-September, tie up the stems and leaves on a warm, dry day and wrap them in black polythene from top to bottom. Pull soil up around the plants, as you would with potatoes. In one month the leaves and stems will be blanched and can be dug up and eaten.

PERENNIALS

The technical definition of a perennial is a plant that lives for more than three years. Perennial veg require less tender loving care than many other vegetables in the way of additional water and nutrients – they put down deep roots, enabling them to access what they need from the soil. In addition, the soil does not have to be repeatedly worked. All you have to do is reserve an area where the plants can be left to grow undisturbed for many years.

ASPARAGUS (*Asparagus officinalis*)

Asparagus has to be one of life's perfect vegetables. Whatever you do with it, it's sublime – steamed, roasted in oil, sautéed in butter, dipped into the yolk of a boiled egg, or tossed into a risotto, it makes an ordinary dish somehow extraordinary. Once it's planted you can more or less forget about it, for it keeps on producing delicious spears for some 20 years – as long as you feed it and keep it weed free. True, you have to wait around three years for your first crop, but just look at the price of it in the shops – this will be well worth the wait.

The plant enjoys a sheltered sunny site and does best in rich, free-draining soil. Prepare the bed in autumn: dig a deep trench and sling in loads of leaf mould and grit. Growing asparagus from seed is a time-consuming business and it is much better to purchase one-year-old crowns instead. Plant these deep in the prepared trenches in spring and space at 45cm (18in) intervals. Each crown should produce between nine and twelve spears per season. Don't pick any spears in the first year and only very sparingly in the second; after that you can forget about exercising restraint. Use a sharp knife to cut them; they can be harvested for up to eight weeks. After harvesting, the plants send up ferny stems, which are essential for the production of healthy spears the following year. Give the asparagus bed protection from frost with fleece or straw. The only possible downside of this vegetable is that, as Marcel Proust observed: 'it transforms my chamber-pot into a flask of perfume'.

FRUITING VEGETABLES

In culinary terms they are vegetables; in botanical terms they can be defined as fruit because they contain seeds. Most are tender and need to be sown under glass.

AUBERGINE (*Solanum melongena*)

Aubergines require a sunny spot to succeed, but in the right conditions they can grow well and there are many interesting varieties and startling colours to try out. Sow seeds under glass in late winter or early spring and prick out into pots when seedlings are large enough to handle. Pinch out the growing tips when they are 30cm (12in) tall and plant out when the first couple of flowers have appeared. Aubergines perform well in grow-bags – two or three plants per bag. Water regularly and feed with a general fertiliser. Pick the aubergines as soon as they have taken on their colour – if left on the plant the skin becomes leathery and the flesh bitter. Take off any fruit that start to form in late summer to help existing fruit to mature properly.

CHILLIES (*Capsicum annuum* var. *annuum,* Longum group)

Chillies are gloriously exotic, but not hard to grow. The peppers come in much more than green or glowing red – there is even a startling purple variety. There are more than 100 varieties to choose from, but not all are suitable for growing out of doors. Grow them as for sweet peppers (see page 41), but sow seeds for hot chillies under glass in late winter – they can take 30 days to germinate. Milder chillies can be sown from late winter to early spring. Stake and tie plants for support; use a cloche or fleece to give extra protection from the wind. Pinch out the growing tips when the plants are 20cm (8in) tall. Plants can be transferred to pots and then on to grow-bags. Chillies can be picked green or left on the plant to colour up; the longer the chilli is left on the plant the hotter it becomes – however this will discourage new fruit from forming.

GLOBE ARTICHOKES (*Cynara scolymus*)

Globe artichokes will give you a fine perennial crop every year; although ideally plants should be replaced after three years as older plants produce fewer and smaller flowers. Theoretically hardy, in practice artichokes may not survive cold northern winters. The plants are beautiful, with silvery leaves and giant blue thistle flowers: however, you do not want the plant to bloom because you want to eat the unopened flower head. Cut the main flower head first and then the side shoots as they appear; a mature plant should produce around six heads. Plants can be sown from seed, but the easy route is to purchase young plants. Seedlings should be placed at 90cm (3ft) intervals and take around 18 months to mature. Mature plants can be divided to increase your crop (see colour section for illustration). They like rich soil and plenty of water; mulch them in the summer and water well.

OKRA (*Abelmoschus esculentus*)

Okra is used in Indian and African cuisine; it is also known as gumbo and lady's fingers. It is tender and struggles to fruit out of doors so, if you really want to grow it, you will need to give it protection with cloches or fleece. Sow seeds under glass at a temperature of around 21–29°C (70–85°F) and keep the seed tray very damp. Transplant the seedlings when big enough to handle and harden off when they are around 30cm (12in) tall, pinching out the growing tips. Plant out in early summer when all fear of frost has passed, having first warmed the soil by covering it with polythene for a fortnight. Space at 60cm (24in) intervals and water frequently. Okra will be ready to crop from 18–20 weeks. Harvest carefully, using a knife or secateurs to remove the pods from the plant as they damage very easily. Large pods become unpleasantly stringy; they don't keep well and need to be used quickly.

SWEETCORN (*Zea mays*)

Fresh sweetcorn is superb – nothing shop-bought can compare. Ideally it should be picked no more than an hour before being cooked and eaten; the sweetness starts turning to starch within hours of picking. Sweetcorn appreciates a sunny, sheltered site with well-drained soil. Dig the plot over the autumn before and add plenty of compost or well-rotted manure. Rake to a fine finish a few weeks before planting and finish with some granular fertiliser – this will get your plants off to a cracking start when they go into the ground. Sow seeds in pots, two per pot, under glass. When the seedlings are around 2cm (¾in) tall, remove the weaker one. Harden off and plant out in blocks in May, spaced at 30cm (12in) intervals. Block planting aids wind germination; the pollen from the male tassels, at the top of the stalk, must reach the female silks, which are lower down the stalk at the top of each ear of corn. There is one silk for every single kernel and if a silk is not pollinated the kernel will not develop. Seeds can be sown directly into the ground in late spring and early summer, but it will help germination if you warm the soil a few weeks in advance by covering it with plastic. There are specific varieties of baby sweetcorn – it is not just an immature cob. These need to be spaced at just 15cm (6in) intervals, but they do take up a lot of room and can produce as little as four cobs per plant. Water well and weed regularly. Corn can be harvested when the tassels at the end of the cob turn brown. If you squeeze a kernel and can see milky liquid, this is another indication that the cob is ripe; if the liquid is watery, the cob needs longer to ripen; and if it is doughy, it is overripe. There is a range of interesting varieties: some are earlies, some middle and some late. In the UK it is safest to grow early varieties, though middles may be fine in the south. Varieties are bred for their sweetness and tender skins, while some are better for drying or for popcorn.

SWEET PEPPERS (*Capsicum annuum* var. *annuum*, Grossum group)

Peppers like a warm environment and are often grown under glass, but some varieties will do quite well out of doors, especially if they are in a sheltered site or close to a sunny wall. Expect to get just three peppers per plant – perhaps a few more if the summer is unusually hot. In all varieties the fruits start off green – they need the sun to develop their final colour. In a poor year they may stay green, but will still be tasty. Sow seeds under glass in trays in mid-spring and transfer to pots when the plant has three true leaves. Harden off the seedlings and plant outside once all danger of frost has passed, spacing them at 45cm (18in) intervals. Keep well watered and mulch to help water retention. Stake the plants and feed with a general fertiliser until the flowers are formed, then switch to a high-potash fertiliser. The peppers will be ready to harvest when they are about 12 weeks old.

TOMATOES *(Lycopersicon esculentum)*

There is nothing more evocative than the glorious smell of tomatoes in the summer. Home-grown fruit has a robust taste and smell that is quite different from those on offer in the supermarket. They need good, fertile soil enriched with plenty of organic matter and a sunny site – grow-bags are very effective. Sow the seeds under glass around eight weeks before they can be planted out, namely in early summer. Pot on when the seedlings have three true leaves; harden off and plant out when all danger of frost has passed, spacing them at 45cm (18in) intervals. Vine tomatoes will need to be supported with canes or string and side shoots should be nipped off. Water regularly – but be aware that both over and under watering are bad for the fruit. Give plants a weekly feed with tomato fertiliser or try a homemade liquid comfrey feed. Fruit can be harvested after 16–20 weeks; pick it as soon as it is ready as it will soften if left on the vine. Once picked, put the fruit in a drawer with a banana if you want to speed up the ripening process, but bear in mind that green tomatoes are fabulous fried and make the most delicious chutney.

ROOT VEGETABLES

Root vegetables are the classic allotment crop, a perfect conjurer's trick where everything happens out of sight and is produced with a flourish of the fork at the end of the season – the magic is all in the growing environment. Root vegetables do a good job of breaking up the soil and deposit plenty of fine roots that improve soil condition.

BEETROOT *(Beta vulgaris)*

Home-grown beetroot bears no resemblance to the pickled, bottled beets found in supermarkets. This really is an underrated vegetable; it's very tasty grated raw and it makes the most wonderful soup. It's been rediscovered by chefs and can be found on good gastro menus all over the country, roasted and baked or grated into slaws and salsas. Globe beetroot crop from May to September; long-rooted varieties can be sown in May and can be stored over winter. There are many different coloured varieties: as well as traditional red, you can grow orange, gold and white. Beetroot is now being dubbed a 'superfood' because the juice has been found to have a significant impact on lowering blood pressure.

Grow in a sunny position. Dig over the plot the autumn before planting and add seaweed fertilisers if you can. Fresh manure or organic material will make roots misshapen so always make sure that organic matter has the opportunity to break down in the soil before beets are planted. Seeds can be sown directly into the soil from April to July, spaced at 30cm (12in) intervals. The root is ready to harvest in 8–16 weeks, depending upon whether you want baby beets or mature beets. If you are desperate for an early crop you can sow seeds under glass and harden off before planting.

BEETROOT AND ORANGE SOUP

Recipes for borscht can be found everywhere, but beetroot and orange soup is equally delicious.

500g (1lb) fresh beetroot
1 onion
Butter
1 litre (2 pints) vegetable stock
1 bay leaf
Juice and grated rind of three fresh oranges
½ teaspoon ground coriander
½ teaspoon ground cinnamon

Wash the beetroot gently until it is clean; remove roots and stalks. Put it through a food processor if you have one, or chop or grate it. Chop the onion and fry very gently in a little butter until translucent. Add the beetroot, vegetable stock, bay leaf and the orange rind and simmer for 20 minutes. Remove the bay leaf. Add the orange juice and the spices, and heat gently. The soup can be served as it is, or can be put through the liquidiser, if preferred.

CARROT *(Daucus carota* subsp. *sativus)*

Fresh carrots taste superb and there is an abundance of interesting varieties to grow, in colours ranging from white to red, and in stump-rooted and long-rooted shapes. Take care to select the right variety for the correct time of year: quick growers are best for spring, main crops for summer and there are autumn/winter varieties that store well. Carrots enjoy a sunny situation and a good light soil; add organic material and sharp sand if you are on clay. Carrot root fly is a problem and, I have to confess, I have not had much luck with carrots without using a barrier such as fleece to keep the pest at bay. Seeds are best sown *in situ*; make successive sowings from early spring to mid-summer. Thin the earlies to a distance of 10cm (4in); main-crop varieties need to be spaced to 8cm (3in). When thinning and weeding, try to work on dull days, or in the evening, as the sun brings out the smell of the carrot foliage and attracts the dreaded carrot root fly. Earlies are ready in 7–10 weeks; main-crop varieties mature in 10–16 weeks. Carrots can be stored successfully in boxes of sand until ready to use.

JERUSALEM ARTICHOKE *(Helianthus tuberosus)*

Jerusalem artichokes have a smoky, strong flavour and, a bit like Marmite, you either love them or hate them – there are no half measures with this root. That committed vegetable fanatic Bob Flowerdew has noted that they do cause an awful lot of wind. The tubers produce hugely tall plants that are equally happy in sun or shade. Plant in early spring, at 30cm (12in) intervals; earth-up when they reach 30cm (12in) in height and stake – they can reach an impressive 3m (10ft). Keep the plants watered in dry weather and pick off any flower buds. The tubers will be ready to eat when the leaves turn brown in winter. The tubers can be left in the soil and dug up as required; a covering of straw over the area in a hard winter will give them some protection.

PARSNIP *(Pastinaca sativa)*

Parsnips sit in the ground for a long time: they are one of the first vegetables to be sown in the open – from early March in the south – and they are not pulled until winter. In fact the roots benefit from being exposed to a good frost to improve their flavour. Parsnips enjoy an open, sunny spot in soil that has been manured the year before for a previous crop – fresh manure will make the roots divide. As parsnips keep the land occupied for a long time, some people sow lettuces or radishes along the drill line to get more use from the space.

Parsnips can be sown under glass in biodegradable modules and then transplanted, or sown directly into the soil – though germination will improve if you cover up the area for a week before planting to warm up the soil. Even so, germination is somewhat unreliable, so make sure you sow the seed thickly. Thin plants or set seedlings at 15–23cm (6–9in) intervals. Hoe regularly to keep the area weed free. Lift parsnips as required: after the first frost they can stay in the soil until February, when they will start to produce leaves if left any longer.

POTATOES (*Solanum tuberosum*)

Growing potatoes, all culinary benefits aside, is a brilliant way to cultivate a strip of land – the soil is regularly turned over, which helps to kill off annual weeds. There are so many varieties to choose from, it's best to keep trying and see which you prefer – some are perfect for boiling, others for baking or even turning into crisps! Potatoes enjoy an open site in well-dug, well-manured soil. Only use disease-resistant potatoes and never grow them near tomatoes: some allotments have had to ban the growing of tomatoes as mosaic virus spreads too easily and contaminates potato crops.

The first process is 'chitting' the seed potatoes, from late January in the south and February in cooler areas. Place them in egg boxes with the 'eyes' facing upwards, in the light, but out of direct sunlight. The potatoes will start to shoot and when these are around 2.5cm (1in) in length they can be planted out, a process that usually takes around six weeks.

First early potatoes can be planted out from mid-March in the south of England and are ready after 12–14 weeks; second earlies are planted out in early April and ready after 15–18 weeks; the main crop is planted towards the end of April and can be lifted after 18–22 weeks.

Place the potatoes, sprouts upward, in a trench 10cm (4in) deep. Space them at 45cm (18in) for earlies and 60cm (2ft) for main crop. If you have comfrey on your plot, pick leaves and let them wilt for a day, then pop them in the base of the trench with some soil and put the potatoes on top – the comfrey leaves will rot to provide a good fertiliser. Infill the trench and pull earth from either side up along the line of the trench. As shoots appear, keep pulling more soil over them for frost protection. Earthing up, as this process is known, also stops light getting to the potatoes, which turns them green and renders them inedible. Water heavily once flowers appear. Cut down foliage on main crop potatoes two weeks before lifting to allow the skin of the potato to toughen up. Dig up potatoes in dry conditions and leave them to dry in the sun for just one hour. Store them in well-ventilated containers in the dark.

SALSIFY *(Tragopogon porrifolius)* AND SCORZONERA *(Scorzonera hispanica)*

Salsify has a distinctive sweet taste; it is commonly known as the oyster plant because of the flavour of its long root. It deserves to be more widely grown. Sow seeds into prepared ground in spring and thin so plants are spaced at 15–25cm (6–10in) intervals. Hoe between the plants to keep the area weed free. The roots will be ready to eat from autumn and can be left in the ground until required. Don't remove all the roots as they will send up shoots in the spring; these are known as chards (not to be confused with Swiss chard) and can be eaten like asparagus. The leaves of the plant are said to be very tasty in salads, though I have yet to try these myself. The flowers are pretty too – all in all it really is very good value for money. Salsify roots are generally boiled in lemon juice or white wine vinegar, which helps to preserve the colour. Eat them like this or sauté them in a little butter after boiling.

Scorzonera is a very similar vegetable, though the flavour is somewhat different and the root is black in colour, but the growing requirements are much the same. They both look a little unappetising, but it is satisfying to grow something that you really can't buy in the shops.

SWEET POTATOES *(Ipomoea batatas)*

Sweet potatoes are increasingly popular and they can be grown in warmer parts of the UK, though it is a bit of a palaver for they cannot abide the cold. A fringe benefit is that the leaves can also be picked and eaten at any time and are delicious sliced and cooked for just a few minutes with garlic in a stir fry. The plant needs a warm, sunny and sheltered spot and the soil must be well worked, with plenty of organic matter and manure dug in, the autumn before planting. Add sand to help drainage.

The seed plants are called slips or cuttings and are best bought from a reputable specialist supplier. Supermarket sweet potatoes have generally been treated with an anti-sprouting agent so you may not be able to get them to grow if you try planting them. The slips should be potted up immediately on arrival. If any have not rooted, pop them into

Wide drills   Narrow drills   *In situ*

Crop rotation

Compost bin

Wigwam cloche

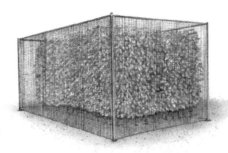

Net cage

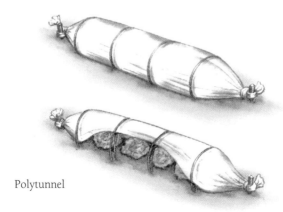

Polytunnel

Jam jars

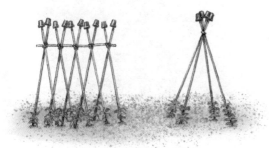

Runner bean
wigwams

Bird scarers

Cordon

Espalier

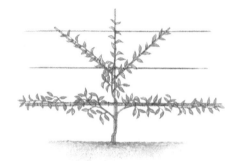

Fan

Layering strawberries

Pruning fruit trees

Raspberry canes

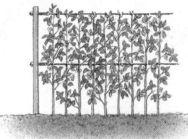

Dividing artichokes

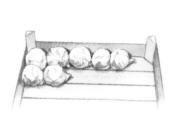

Storing fruit

1

2

Storing tubers

3

an unheated propagator, or cover the pot with a plastic bag and keep them in full light until the roots appear. Grow them in pots in a frost-free environment and plant them out in early June – in most areas they will still require the protection of either fleece or a cloche. Keep them well watered.

Sweet potatoes are from the same genus as the garden favourite Morning Glory, with a similar twisting vine growth pattern. Advice varies as to whether the leaves should be trained to go upwards to allow warmth and light to get to the soil, or whether the leaves should be allowed to spread out to suppress weeds. Tubers can be lifted from the end of August or when the leaves start to yellow.

LEGUMES

Legumes are kitchen garden and allotment favourites for they are, in the most part, easy to grow, productive plants – the more you pick, the more you get. Nitrogen-fixing nodules on their roots are beneficial to the soil: when clearing the spent crops, cut the plants off at ground level and leave the root systems behind to enrich the soil. Rotation is therefore important (pests and diseases aside), as nitrogen deposits in the soil would make subsequent leguminous crops leafy and unproductive. However, other plants, such as brassicas or leafy greens, would appreciate the nitrogen in the soil. Legumes enjoy an open, sunny site. Dig the soil over in February or March, good and early to allow it to settle, and incorporate organic matter. Most legumes need support, so put pea sticks or hazel twigs in place. Many can be planted *in situ*, but always put three or four seeds in at a time, as you may well lose some seeds or seedlings to pests.

RUNNER BEANS *(Phaseolus coccineus)*

In my book you can't really call yourself an allotment holder
if you're not growing runner beans! It's hard to go wrong with
them, but they do benefit from good soil preparation and
plenty of water. Seeds or seedlings cannot be planted out
until all danger of frost has passed, so time your sowing
accordingly. Early sowings under glass will give plants a
four-week head start, but the plant has a high germination rate
so you will do just as well planting straight into the ground in
late May. Always pop a few spare seeds at the end of the rows
to fill any gaps that occur. If late frosts are threatened you can
always put plastic-bottle cloches around your seedlings for
protection. Mulch to help moisture retention. Tie the plants
on to their supports as they grow and nip off the tips when
they reach the top of the canes. Pick beans every few days;
they start appearing in late June and keep cropping for a
couple of months. They freeze very well.

FRENCH BEANS *(Phaseolus vulgaris)*

With French beans you get three vegetables in one. The whole
pods can be eaten young, but if left to mature the beans
within develop into flageolet beans that
feature in so many Italian dishes – left
longer still, they grow to become the
mighty haricot. There are three
varieties of French bean: dwarf,
haricot and climbing (which
requires staking). All varieties
can be eaten green. They are
a little finicky to begin with:

seeds need to be sown in a greenhouse and hardened off
before planting out. Never sow seeds or plant seedlings if the
weather is cold or wet – they can be killed off by the lightest
frost. Space plants at 30cm (12in) intervals. Ensure that the
plant is supported if the variety so requires – some can reach
1.8m (6ft) – and pinch out the tips at intervals to promote
flowering. Keep the plants weed free and water regularly.
Some varieties will begin to crop as early as eight weeks after
sowing; the more you pick, the more they produce! If you
have grown haricot-size pods, leave the pods on the plants
until they are fully ripened. Cut the whole plant in the
autumn and hang them up to dry. When the pods are
crispy, shell the beans and spread them out on a tray
to dry fully.

PEAS (Pisum sativum)

The garden pea has many varieties and incorporates three
forms of this popular vegetable; mangetout, sugar snap (with
a fuller, juicier, crisper pod), or the classic petit pois or garden
pea (petit pois being younger, smaller peas). Dig over your pea
plot and incorporate plenty of well-rotted manure or compost
into the soil a month before planting. One week before
planting, rake in a top dressing of general fertiliser. Early
crops need to be started off under glass and hardened off
before being transplanted, but from late spring seeds can be
planted directly into the soil, though not if it is wet or cold.
Space at 8–20cm (3–8in) intervals and support the plants with
twiggy pea sticks as they grow. Sow seed fortnightly to ensure
a continual supply throughout the summer; an autumn crop
can be sown in July. Water the plants well, especially in dry
weather – a mulch may help stop the soil from drying out.

It is better to pick your crop before it is fully mature – young peas taste better than old bullets. Both birds and mice will be attracted to them!

BROAD BEANS *(Vicia faba)*

Broad beans are a staple in all kinds of Italian dishes. They have a juicy snap when picked young and tender, totally unlike the tinned sort. There are many varieties offering a choice of colour and height. Early-sowing, long-pod varieties contain eight seeds; shorter varieties, Windsors, are sown later in the season and contain four seeds – some growers maintain they have a superior flavour. Make regular sowings of seeds on a monthly basis to ensure successive crops, starting in late winter or early spring. Further into the year, they can be sown directly into the soil. Broad beans enjoy a well-dug soil, so dig over in advance. Space plants at 15cm (6in) intervals, in staggered rows around 23cm (9in) apart; support with 1m (3ft) hazel twigs and string. The plants should begin to crop from May; pick the pods when they are around 5cm (2in) long to eat whole, or when the seed shape is visible in the pod for beans alone. A 6m (20ft) row will produce around 18kg (40lb) of beans.

BRASSICAS

It has to be said, unglamorous though they are, that brassicas are solid, reliable, healthy vegetables. They have a long growing season – seed is planted in spring and many of the vegetables overwinter in the ground before cropping – and they are an allotment staple, their sculptural shapes defining the productivity of the winter allotment. The downside is that they are horribly prone to clubroot disease and great care must be taken with crop rotation and the positioning of their immediate neighbours. These plants actually prefer a partially shaded site, which is a real boon when most fruit and vegetables have a preference for sunshine. They require a fertile, well-drained soil and it is important that compost and well-rotted manure is dug in the autumn before planting. Immediately before planting, the soil should be raked and trodden repeatedly – as if you were preparing to lay a lawn – to remove air pockets. Brassicas will not tolerate an acid soil, so you may have to add lime; the ideal pH level is between 6.5 and 7.5. Some plants may need support or earthing up, to help prevent root rock. Birds enjoy the seedlings and can be a nuisance – CDs hung on strings can act as a deterrent.

BROCCOLI *(Brassica oleracea, Italica* group)

Broccoli likes a sunny spot, but will tolerate partial shade and has a preference for a rich, well-dug, heavy soil, though this must be done well in advance – preferably the autumn before the crop is planted. It will not tolerate too much wind, so a sheltered site is best. Assorted varieties can be sown at different times: green broccoli, or calabrese, is sown under cover in early April or *in situ* from early May and harvested in the autumn; purple and white sprouting varieties are sown in mid-April and harvested in the spring. Calabrese hates root disturbance, so should be grown in pots, but sprouting broccoli grows very readily and can be sown in seed trays or a seed bed. Calabrese should be spaced at 50cm (20in) intervals; sprouting broccoli at 60cm (2ft) intervals. The latter benefits from the support of stakes and string to stop it being rocked by winds in winter.

BRUSSELS SPROUTS (*Brassica oleracea, Gemmifera* group)

Despite the bad press they get, these for me are the king of vegetables – though they are truly vile if overcooked. I also happen to think that Brussels sprouts are beautifully sculptural, a form of exotic plant installation with that tight green bobbled stem and overblown stem tops. A range of varieties will allow you to produce crops from autumn right through to spring and offer exotic alternatives such as red sprouts. They appreciate an open site and are content in shade, but cannot cope with wind – they are, after all, peculiarly top heavy.

Dig over the soil well in advance – ideally it will have been well manured for a previous crop – and spread some lime. The earliest seeds can be sown mid-March to mid-April in a sheltered seed bed, and thinned. Transplant when they reach 10–15cm (4–6in) or are six weeks old, spacing them at 50–60cm (20–24in). Keep the area weed free; hand weeding is a good idea because a hoe can damage their shallow roots. Water in dry weather, earth up the stems in autumn in sandy soil and stake, if necessary. Pigeons can be a nuisance – try hanging CDs on strings nearby as a deterrent – but some people are forced to net their crop. Keep an eye open for caterpillars and pick them off as soon as you see them.

If you like large sprouts then take off the growing tip of the plant in September, though this will decrease your overall harvest. Sprouts are ready to pick when they are small and tight. They taste sweeter after the first frost. Pick from the bottom of the stem upwards and use a knife to cut them off – snapping can damage the stem. The stem tops can also be eaten. Clear the site thoroughly at the end of the season.

CAULIFLOWER (*Brassica oleracea, Botrytis* group)

Cauliflowers are not the easiest vegetables to grow. They
like a sunny spot and good rich, heavy soil, ideally one that
contained a legume crop the previous year – in which case
no manure will need to be added. They require plenty of
water to succeed – drought can cause terrible setbacks.
There are numerous varieties that can be grown to produce
a year-round harvest, plus exciting new colourful varieties
in orange, green and purple.

Seeds of summer varieties should be sown in modules
under glass in late winter. Harden them off and transplant out
in early spring, spaced at 45cm (18in) intervals. These will be
ready to harvest after around 16–20 weeks. Autumn and
winter crops should be sown in late spring and transplanted
to the main bed around six weeks later, spaced as above.
Check throughout the growing season for caterpillars and
their eggs – remove these and squish them. These later
crops take longer to reach maturation; they can be harvested
after 40–50 weeks. Cut heads before they get too mature.
Cauliflowers are like courgettes: they can surprise you with a
sudden growth spurt when you least expect it and can go over
and spoil. Storing is a bit of a nightmare: cauliflowers need to
be hung upside down in a cool shed, and even so they will
only last around three weeks. Fortunately, if you have a
bumper crop, the florets freeze beautifully.

CABBAGE (*Brassica oleracea, Capitata* group)

The glorious thing about cabbage is its many and varied forms
– red cabbage, white cabbage, Savoy cabbage, and spring,
summer and winter varieties – all taste quite different, have

different culinary uses and are easy to grow. They enjoy an open, sunny site and well-drained alkaline soil.

Different varieties are all grown in the same way: adjust your timings to the relevant season and make successive sowings for continual crops. Seeds should be planted under glass in trays or modules, and seedlings transplanted to the main bed when they have three or four leaves. Sow summer varieties in late spring and plant out at 30–45cm (12–18in) intervals; you can start harvesting them after 20 weeks. Sow autumn and winter varieties in late spring and transplant in early summer, spaced at 50cm (20in) intervals; start harvesting after 26–30 weeks. Sow spring varieties in the main bed from mid to late summer. Space them at 30cm (12in) intervals for cabbage heads; if you want greens, plant them at half the distance. They'll be ready for cropping in 20–35 weeks. Water plants regularly once the heads have formed and pull earth up to the base of the plants to give protection from frost. After the cabbage is harvested, sprouts grow around where the head was removed: these are incredibly delicious, a real gourmet treat – sauté in butter, with a little water to keep everything moist, until just tender.

CHINESE CABBAGE (Brassica rapa, Pekinensis group) AND PAK CHOI (Brassica rapa, Chinensis group)

There are two varieties of Chinese cabbage, the loose-leafed type and its tighter-leafed relative, pak choi. Both varieties like an open, sunny site with moisture-retentive soil and both hate root disturbance. Sow seeds *in situ* and thin according to the final size of plant you require. I prefer the smaller, tighter leaves so space plants at approximately 15cm (6in) intervals;

for larger plants leave larger gaps. Pak choi can be sown from mid-June to late August and plants will be ready to crop in just three weeks. Chinese cabbage seeds should be sown after midsummer and spaced at intervals of 30cm (12in). It can be cropped after 6–10 weeks. Sow at fortnightly intervals for successive crops. It is possible to produce earlier and later crops, but these tend to be far less successful.

KALE (*Brassica oleracea, Acephala* group)

Curly kale is *de rigueur* on all good restaurant menus in early spring. It has a strong flavour that is not to everyone's taste – my children would rather pull their own teeth than eat it – but it is much improved for being home grown, when the youngest leaves can be harvested and eaten quickly. It does not store well and the old leaves can get unpleasantly bitter, which is why the home-grown product is so superior. Curly kale is one of my favourite vegetables and is ready to eat in the autumn, much earlier than its smooth-leafed relative.

Plant the seeds in a nursery bed. On germination thin seedlings to 8cm (3in) intervals and transplant them when they reach 15cm (6in) in height. Alternatively, sow the seeds *in situ* in April and thin to space plants at 45cm (18in) intervals. Remove any yellowing leaves, earth-up the stems and tread around to provide support. The plant will be ready for harvesting after 26–40 weeks. Start by stripping young leaves from the crown in November: this encourages side shoots to develop, which can be harvested from February to May. Curly kale doesn't have a high water content so the leaves don't collapse like other leaf greens. The stems are often best cooked for a few minutes before the leaf.

KOHLRABI *(Brassica oleracea, Gongyloides* group)

This vegetable looks somewhat like a miniature version of the Millennium Dome. I think it is a bit of a novelty, but trying out new produce is what having an allotment is all about. It enjoys an open, sunny situation and a light, sandy soil. Sow the seeds *in situ* from mid-spring to mid-summer and thin to 18cm (7in). The root can be harvested in mid-autumn when it should have grown roughly to the size of a tennis ball.

RADISH *(Raphanus sativus)*

Everyone is familiar with the small but fast-growing, peppery vegetable used in salads. Less well known is the winter radish, which will grow quite big and can be treated much like its relative the turnip in culinary terms, or finely sliced and used in stir fries. Summer radishes can be sown directly into the soil; for successive crops repeat sow every three weeks. The plant enjoys a sunny spot, but equally likes cool conditions so it will grow happily among taller plants such as peas and beans. It's a brilliant starter vegetable for children; they can sow the seed in April and within five weeks will be unearthing their crop. If summer radish is left in the ground too long it gets very peppery and loses its crispness.

Winter radishes, which come in both red and white varieties, have much larger roots, so they require a fine seed bed. Sow the seed in late July or early August, and thin out to 15cm (6in) intervals. Plants will be ready to harvest after 10–12 weeks, though they can be left in the ground until required, as long as their crown is protected with straw or fleece. Alternatively, lift and store in a box in a cool but frost-free environment.

SWEDE (*Brassica napus, Napobrassica* group)

Swede is a much underrated vegetable whose reputation has
been tarnished by the soggy mash that school dinner ladies
used to slop on the plate, and (for feeble southerners) it has
a dubious association with haggis. It is delicious roasted and
sprinkled with Parmesan. Alternatively, boil it with potatoes,
strain, and mash the potato and swede together – adding
butter, milk and seasoning, or cream, if you are feeling
decadent. Cook a little cabbage separately, stir it into
the mash mix and you have a hearty dish of Colcannon.

    Swedes appreciate an open, sunny site and a fertile soil.
Along with most brassicas, they cannot cope with freshly
manured ground: either plant where the ground was well
manured for the previous crop or dig in well-rotted manure
and organic matter six months in advance. Sow the seeds
in situ in late spring in the south, or a little later, in early
summer, in the north. Thin seedlings to 30cm (12in) apart,
and water regularly. Roots can be cropped after 20–26 weeks;
leave them in the ground and lift as required. Alternatively,
store in boxes in a cool, well-ventilated place.

TURNIP (*Brassica rapa, Rapifera* group)

Turnip is a resolutely old-fashioned vegetable. It has been
popular since time immemorial because it is easy to grow and
a fast cropper, but suffers from a bit of an image problem. It is
positively delicious baked in the oven for a couple of hours
and equally tasty when roasted. You can also try boiling it;
first peel and cut into chunks, mash when cooked and cover
with a white sauce, or just pour a little cream over and put
lots of black pepper on top. White- and yellow-fleshed

varieties are available. Sow seeds *in situ* and sow monthly for successive crops. Thin plants to 23cm (9in) intervals – larger seedlings can be cooked as tasty greens. Water regularly: if the turnips become dry, the root will split. The crop can be lifted after 20–26 weeks. A 3m (10ft) row will produce around 5kg (11lb), which is probably just enough turnips for one year – if you like them enough.

THE ONION FAMILY

At Goodnestone Gardens in Kent there is a magnificent kitchen garden and in late summer the rows of onions are pulled and left to dry in the sun – a better advertisement for the joy of onion growing does not exist. Onions are culinary essentials and they are easy to grow. All alliums like a fertile soil, but it shouldn't be too rich; don't manure the soil just before planting; this should always be done a few months in advance. Onions have fringe benefits – they are believed to give some degree of disease resistance to nearby plants.

GARLIC *(Allium sativum)*

Garlic will grow easily enough in a dry, sunny spot, but it doesn't like to be too wet. It comes in different strengths of flavour and colours – white, pink and purple. Dig soil over prior to planting, then make holes, just 2.5–5cm (1–2in) deep and 10cm (4in) apart – you can use a dibber for this. Plant the cloves in autumn, blunt end down, with the neck of the clove poking above the soil. You can use garlic bought from your supermarket or greengrocer for planting out. The plants don't need much attention: weed around them carefully and only water if they get very dry. Some people advise a feed of liquid fertiliser in mid March, but this is not essential. If the garlic throws up a flowering stem, cut this back by around half well before it gets to flower – this encourages the bulb to grow fat. The garlic is ready to dig up when the leaves start to yellow the following summer – generally around August, but it can be earlier. Bulbs can be dried out of doors in the sunshine or indoors, but don't let them get wet. Garlic can be eaten 'green' for a sweeter flavour.

LEEKS *(Allium porrum)*

Leeks are a classic allotment crop, sometimes produced to freakishly outsized proportions for competitions, but very easy to grow if you're not looking for perfect specimens. Comfort yourself in the knowledge that monster veg grown for size alone often taste vile! Different varieties mature at different times: tall, slim, early varieties such as 'King Richard', are ready by late summer; main crops such as 'Toledo' can be pulled in winter, and lates, such as the pretty 'Alaska', in spring. Planting a range of varieties will extend your growing season.

Sow the seeds under glass; the early varieties can be started off in late winter, the other varieties can be sown directly into a seed bed in late spring and early summer. Harden off seedlings when they are 20cm (8in) tall and about as thick as a pencil then plant out between June and August. Make a hole 15cm (6in) deep and drop the plant into it, but do not backfill with soil. Instead, water in the seedling so that the soil settles itself around the plant. Space plants at 15–30cm (6–12in) intervals. Weed and water regularly and mulch – piling the earth up against the stem by degrees as it grows to keep them white. Try to stop soil from going down into the leaves – it's infuriating when you are cleaning them and can introduce pests and diseases. Plants can be harvested from mid-autumn to late spring; hardy varieties can be left in the soil until they are needed

ONIONS *(Allium cepa)*

Onions are easy to grow and although they can be prone to some pests and diseases, they are still a worthwhile crop. They can be grown from sets (small immature bulbs), which is a fairly foolproof method, though more expensive than seed. There are two principal taste options when it comes to choosing varieties: the stronger-flavoured onions and the milder, often larger ones which are sometimes called European onions. 'Stuttgarter', 'Sturon' and 'Yellow Globe' are good, pungent onions, or try growing a red variety such as 'Red Wethersfield'. Different varieties have different sowing seasons: many can be grown from seed in spring, but Japanese onions, or short-day varieties, are sown in late summer for harvesting the following summer – well before the usual onion harvest. By growing both, you will have onions for most of the year.

Onions like a sunny site with a rich, light soil. Plant the sets in shallow holes, leaving the tip showing, from mid-winter to early spring, and space at 10cm (4in) intervals. Seeds can be grown in early spring under glass and transplanted out in late spring. Alternatively, sow seeds *in situ* at this time, but you may not get such good results. Thin the seedlings so that they are spaced at 10cm (4in) intervals. If you leave a larger space you will get bigger onions, but these do not keep so well as the smaller ones.

Onion fly can cause difficulties: if it's a problem on your plot, steer clear of seed and plant sets instead. Onions are ready to be lifted when the tops have turned over and died back – never bend the leaves over to hasten this process, it can cause neck rot. Use a fork to gently lift them and, if it is sunny, leave them to dry on the soil. If it is wet bring them in to dry; they can be stored in single layers in boxes or plaited into long strings, which allows the air to circulate around them to stop diseases or rot. My method is to take a long loop of stout string and hang it from something sturdy. Then I use onions whose leaves are still slightly floppy – this is too difficult once the leaves are completely dry. Starting with the larger onions first, tie two together at the base with their own leaves, then wind the leaves of each onion around the string. Continue with more onions in pairs and try to make sure that each onion is not quite resting on the one below.

SHALLOTS *(Allium cepa, Aggregatum* group)

Shallots have a sweeter, milder flavour than onions and can be grown from seed or, more simply, as sets or cloves. Plant the latter in mid-winter in a shallow depression filled with sand. Pop the sets in and leave the tips showing, spaced at 15cm (6in) intervals. Birds are inclined to pull them out – you may need to put a little tunnel of chicken wire over them if this is a problem. If the neck of the shallot pokes out in spring, it may need some frost protection – a layer of fleece is ideal. Keep the area free of weeds, water regularly and give the shallots a feed in spring. Seeds should be sown in early spring and the plants hardened off prior to planting out in late spring. Seed-sown shallots need to be fed and watered regularly until the summer. Lift them when the leaves have withered: store in a dry place and reserve some sets for next year's crop.

Spring onions or salad onions
(Allium cepa)

Spring onions, also known as scallions, deserve to be far more widely used than as a mere seasonal addition to a summer salad in traditional English style. They play a large part in Japanese and Asian cookery and as a result are becoming an important crop. Sow seeds in drills from early spring to late summer and thin to 3cm (1¼in). The plants will be ready to eat in 8–10 weeks; for successive crops, keep sowing seeds every 3–4 weeks. Late sowings in August and September will produce a crop by early the following spring, but you will need to choose a special hardy winter variety.

Welsh onions *(Allium fistulosum)*

This plant's origins are not in the least Welsh – it is thought to come from Siberia or China. It is useful if you like Asian cuisine and tastes somewhat like a chive. The leaves are hollow and it does not develop a bulb. Seeds sown in spring will be ready by the autumn, and those sown in the summer will be ready the following spring. It can be cultivated much like the onion, but it is a perennial and is known as the everlasting onion because it keeps on increasing. If you leave a few onions in the ground you'll always have a supply.

THE PUMPKIN FAMILY

I have a great fondness for this family of vegetables. With the exception of cucumbers, they will obligingly grow *in situ* from seed and can reach record-breaking proportions.

COURGETTE OR MARROW *(Cucurbita pepo)*

A courgette (or zucchini) is just a baby marrow. If you don't pick these babies at just the right time, they suddenly transform, Hulk-like, into pumped-up, outsized marrows. Every year I aim to grow courgettes but every year I take prizes for my mighty marrows. How they get to be so big, so fast, I'll never know. It's all in the timing! There is a number of varieties, both in trailing and bush form, and colours of green or yellow. You can sow the seeds under glass in spring; pop two into a pot at a time and then transplant after hardening off. Better still, sow them straight into the ground later in the season; again pop two into each spot and remove the weaker plant when leaves appear. Space bush plants at 90cm (3ft) intervals and trailing plants at a distance of 1.8m (6ft) – these will need to be supported with stakes. Feed every two weeks with a liquid feed and water well. Pick the courgettes as soon as you feel they are large enough.

Courgettes are delicious and fantastically adaptable: they can be boiled, sautéed, roasted, made into soups or added to simple pasta dishes. The flowers are edible: if you are getting a glut of fruit, you may want to use the flowers up to buy yourself a breathing space. All you have to do is wash them, leave to drain, then dip them into a batter mix and fry.

Marrows are good too – but they are so big, just one goes an awful long way. Try roasting or stuffing them. I like them best stuffed with other tasty veg that have been chopped up small and roasted.

300g (10½oz) grated courgette

3 teaspoons chopped parsley

3 teaspoons snipped chives

3 teaspoons chopped mint

3 eggs

3 tablespoons natural yoghurt

4 soup spoons olive oil

100g (3½oz) pine nuts

2 teaspoons baking powder

1 teaspoon curry powder

Salt and pepper

250g (9oz) plain flour

Set the oven temperature to 250°C (gas mark 9). Mix all the
ingredients together and place in a greased loaf tin. Bake for
10 minutes, then lower the temperature to 200°C (gas mark
6) and cook for a further 45 minutes.

CUCUMBERS *(Cucumis sativus)*

Cucumbers grow beautifully in a greenhouse, but some new
varieties are equipped to withstand the rigours of outdoor life.
Sow out-of-doors species under glass in late spring about
1.2cm (½in) deep on their edges. They can't withstand frost,
so plan ahead and start seeds off about four weeks before the
last frosts are due. In addition, they don't like root disturbance
and are best sown in biodegradable modules. Keep seeds
reasonably warm and don't over water as they easily succumb
to damping off. Begin to harden off plants once they have
three proper leaves.

Dig a trench a few weeks before the plants are large enough to be planted out; fill it with compost and well-rotted manure and pull the soil back so that there is now a mound of soil. Plant the cucumbers at 75cm (30in) intervals. Protect them if the weather turns cold and water them regularly, but not directly on top of the plant. Provide support for trailing varieties and nip out the growing tip when it has reached the top of its support. When you plant the seedling, ensure that the top of the soil is slightly below the level it was at in the pot; this helps to avoid neck rot. Don't leave cucumbers on the plant – cut them off as soon as they reach a suitable size to encourage further cropping. A very small cucumber is a gherkin: in Algerian restaurants they serve tiny whole ones to eat raw – crisp and refreshing.

PUMPKINS AND SQUASHES (*Cucurbita maxima* and *Cucurbita* species)

I have a passion for anything vaguely sweet so I love these vegetables. There are so many different varieties to choose from, and the flesh of each one tastes slightly different. Some of them are exquisite works of art that look fabulous – and taste sublime when halved and baked in the oven.

Squashes are subdivided into winter and summer varieties. There is actually no real difference between them: the fruit of summer squash is eaten when immature; the fruit of winter squash is eaten when it is fully mature. Winter squash are easier to store, doubtless in part due to their thick skins, caused by a longer maturation period than summer squashes. Just think how sturdy a pumpkin is until it is hollowed out for Halloween, then it starts to collapse in just a few days. Winter squash can also be eaten early, like courgettes.

All squash seeds like the same treatment: sow them on their edges in deep pots. Prepare large planting holes. Dig a hole around 45cm (18in) in diameter and depth, mix the soil with the same quantity of compost or well-rotted manure and backfill the hole, leaving a mound. Harden off the seedlings and plant out, around 1m (3ft 3in) apart. Summer squash seeds should be planted in early spring when all danger of frost has passed. The fruit can be harvested once it has reached around 15cm (6in) in length. Patty Pan is one of the best-known varieties. Winter squashes and pumpkins seeds can be sown in individual pots in late spring, or sown *in situ* when the weather is warm enough. Don't over water these plants once they are established, but feed with a liquid fertiliser every fortnight. Remove the growing tip of the plant and support fruit with straw.

To establish whether a fruit is ripe, tap it – if it sounds hollow, it's ready to eat. Winter squash should be stored for a fortnight to ripen and harden off in a warm room with good circulation. Take care when selecting your pumpkin variety: you can get them for eating or for Hallowe'en – in which case they can grow to giant proportions. Summer squash can be steamed, sautéed and casseroled; varieties to try include 'Scallopini' and 'Custard White'. Winter squash varieties include 'Buttercup', 'Carnival Squash', 'Sweet Dumpling' and 'Delicata', which all taste a little like sweet potato.

PUMPKIN PIE

This is an American favourite for Thanksgiving and Christmas – basically a pastry shell filled with a sort of pumpkin custard.

This recipe was given to me by the owner of a B & B in Santa Monica, California.

Make 500g (1lb) sweet shortcrust pastry and mix in 40g
     (1½oz) crushed pecans – or cheat and add pecans to
     readymade pastry.
500g (1lb) pumpkin flesh cut into chunks (use a small
     pumpkin, such as 'Jackpot', 'Spirit' or 'Trick or Treat')
2 large eggs and one extra yolk
75g (3oz) soft brown sugar
1 teaspoon ground cinnamon
1 teaspoon ground cloves (optional)
1 teaspoon ground allspice (optional)
½ level teaspoon ground nutmeg
½ teaspoon ground ginger
275ml (10fl oz) double cream

Preheat the oven to 180°C (gas mark 4). Steam the pumpkin, then set aside in a colander to drain – you want to remove as much water as possible. Use a blender or mash to a purée in a bowl. (If you have time, leave the purée to drain overnight to reduce the water content further.)

Whisk the eggs and egg yolk together in a bowl. Place the sugar, spices and cream in a saucepan and gently bring to simmering point, pour over the egg mixture and whisk gently. Add the pumpkin purée and whisk some more.

Pour into the pastry case and bake in the oven for 35–40 minutes. It should remain a little soft in the centre. Serve warm or cool, with cream or ice cream.

FRUIT

Nothing beats the taste of home-grown fruit – it doesn't matter how good the supermarket offer is, it will never come close to bettering your own fruit in a blind tasting. Home-grown fruit smells wonderful, oozes juice and has a texture all of its own that is part of the whole sensual experience. Apples are crisp and juicy, gooseberries are firm and sweetly acidic, raspberries are beautiful little sculptures with not a trace of gooey mush.

All fruit can be grown on an allotment, though some sites have rules prohibiting the growing of fruit trees – they do not want them to grow so large that they shade other plots. But there are always ways around such restrictions. Remember that the trees you see in modern fruit orchards are always small, so that the fruit can be picked by hand without the use of a ladder. Regular autumn pruning will result in dear little trees that will produce a fabulous crop. See colour section for illustration. A dwarf apple tree can produce around 7kg (15lb) of fruit in a good year.

If trees are strictly forbidden then you can always try growing tree fruit on cordons (angled wires), espaliers or fans. See colour section for illustrations. While not quite as productive as a tree, they look simply stunning all year round and, in my book, where gardening is in part a visual pleasure, such controlled and architectural growth is always attractive, particularly when studded with pears, plums or apples in the fruiting season.

Growing fruit is far less labour intensive than growing vegetables, which people often focus on initially. In fact, getting started with fruit is a very good way to begin. You are establishing a long-term crop – fruit trees can be productive for many years and, gooseberries and currants can last for 20 years. Some take a couple of years to establish themselves before fruiting begins. If an allotment is very run down and weedy you can always partially clear it and plant an area with fruit bushes (surround them with old carpet to kill off the weeds), while you then concentrate on clearing an area for the more labour-intensive vegetables.

The other attraction for a lazy gardener like myself is that fruit is blessedly easy to grow. Bushes and plants appreciate a little care when planted, but aside from that they don't need to be replaced annually, will tolerate less fertile soil and they're not very labour intensive. Plant them, pick them and prune them – far less strenuous than double digging and endless feeding. As a general rule they appreciate a slightly acid soil and enjoy a warm spot. If you get a hard frost in spring when they are flowering, your crop will be lost – so thinking about their position, avoiding frost pockets and giving them a little protection will pay handsome dividends. If you live in the north, or have problems with frost, select varieties that flower and fruit later in the season. Store the fruit wrapped individually in boxes, or in bags (see colour section for illustration).

Fruit can essentially be divided into two main categories: soft fruit and fruit trees. Then there are glorious anomalies such as rhubarb, which is technically a vegetable, but which is included in this section, though tomatoes, which are technically a fruit, are not. I'm working on popular principle here rather than technical correctness – if you eat it for dessert then let's call it a fruit.

GROWING FRUIT TREES

Working on the rule that 'small is beautiful' in allotment terms, it is best to buy half-standard trees. These have trunks around 1.2–1.8m (4–6ft) tall, making the tree easy to prune and the crop easy to pick. Fruit bushes are even smaller: apples and pears have just 70cm (28in) tall stems, while cherries and plums have stems of just 1m (3ft 3in) tall. Such types have been grafted onto dwarfing stock to keep their growth firmly in check.

Young trees recover from transplanting faster than more mature ones; bare-rooted one-year-old whips (available in November) are the most reasonable to buy; bush trees are purchased at between one and two years of age. Slightly older trees that have been pruned into early shape by the nursery will give you a head start in terms of crops. Half standards are three years of age and standards three to four years old. Be sensible in your selection – a mulberry tree that forms a huge tree and takes years to fruit is never going to be a good choice.

ESPALIERS

An espalier has five or six tiers of horizontal branches at right angles to the main stem and spaced at 30cm (1ft) intervals. It is possible to purchase one-storey espaliers, known as stepovers, which can be planted around the edges of beds to form a low fruiting fence. Espaliers are best suited for growing apples and pears. Fan-shaped trees do as the name suggests – branches fan out from the main stem. They are best for plums, cherries, figs and apricots. Ideally, buy espaliers and fans that are three to four years of age.

A cordon is a tree that has a single stem. The side growths are pruned back very hard to encourage the growth of fruiting spurs all along the stem. It is planted upright, but trained to grow at an angle of 45 degrees. There are various complex cordon-growing options, including double horizontal, double stem and triple stem, but start with basics. Cordons should be two years old at purchase. They will need the support of post and wire throughout their life. Nurseries that specialise in fruit can give you the best advice on varieties to suit your plot.

FRUIT TREES

Growing your own fruit from trees allows you to steer away from obvious varieties, to explore new taste sensations and to experiment with traditional and rare varieties. For example, there are around 2,500 varieties of apple, over 500 varieties of pear and 300 varieties of plum. The choice available in the supermarkets and grocers is severely curtailed and a large percentage will be imported. Commercial growers are looking to produce fruit with a long shelf-life and taste is less of a consideration. With your own trees you can explore the full range of offer.

APPLE (*Malus domestica*)

Put bluntly, the apple is one of the easiest crops to grow – particularly cooking apples. There really is no excuse not to be growing one of our very oldest fruits in some form or another – there are more than two thousand varieties to choose from. Some of our most popular dessert varieties are harder to grow,

so don't make life difficult – after all Cox's Orange Pippin are available by the tonne in the supermarket. What you can't buy are some of the older varieties, such as Blenheim Orange, which reliably produce the most delicious fruit and offer a delightful change from the ubiquitous Pippin.

Apple trees need to be cross pollinated by bees to fruit, so it is advisable to grow two varieties that blossom at the same time. Relying on another apple tree on a plot nearby will be no use if it flowers a whole month earlier or later than yours. Apples fall into between four and seven pollination groups so ask for advice when you buy your trees.

It is also important to understand whether your tree is tip bearing or spur bearing; tip-bearing trees require less attention, but as these often grow into large trees you are more likely to have a spur-bearing type. These need to have their branches shortened to promote fruiting between November and March. Fruit needs to be thinned on large trees, but on dwarf trees, espaliers and cordons you should not have to bother. Apples are ready for picking when the apple comes easily away from the tree with a lift and a twist.

CHERRY (Prunus avium)

Cherries might seem an ideal fruit to grow on an allotment for they really do not travel well. Like the mulberry, they used to be impossible to grow on allotments because at least two trees were needed for cross pollination and they took up a lot of space. However new self-fertile bush cultivars have been grafted on to Gisela, a dwarfing rootstock, and can produce up to 10kg (22lb) of fruit. These make cherries a more practical allotment choice, although even self-fertile plants benefit from having a suitable cross-pollinator nearby.

Cherries are still not a viable option for everyone, as they like warmth and do best in the south in warm, sheltered spots with a slightly acid soil (between 6.0 and 6.8). The trees will not tolerate exposed sites, standing in water or frost pockets. They can be demanding: when fruiting they respond well to reflective material being placed on surrounding ground; they benefit from being covered with polythene in heavy rain when fruit is ripening (they absorb the water and their skin will split); and they must be netted to protect the fruit from the birds. However if you only have one or two small trees then this isn't so much hassle for a very rich reward.

Trees benefit from annual pruning in April when in leaf, to keep the structure light, airy and cone shaped. Formative pruning is undertaken in August and is designed to remove older, thicker branches and shoots that are growing upwards or downwards. Once the plant has been established for one year, apply a top dressing of fertiliser every winter.

PLUM, GAGE AND DAMSON (Prunus domestica, P. domestica and P. insititia)

Plums are delightfully easy to grow and hugely rewarding in terms of crop. They require a warm, sheltered site as they flower early in the season and the blossom can be damaged by late spring frosts. Plum trees can grow quite large, but Pixy, the new semi-dwarf rootstock, has made the fruit perfectly well suited to the allotment. You can get as much as 17kg (37lb) of fruit from a half standard. If you have room for only one plant, choose a variety that is self fertile.

It is important to prune trees only when the weather is warm. Plums are very susceptible to silver-leaf disease and are most vulnerable to this entering via pruning cuts in autumn and winter.

Greengages and damsons are rarely found for sale in supermarkets and greengrocers. For the allotment grower, both are now available on dwarf rooting stock. Greengages are a delicious yellow-fleshed, green- or yellow-skinned variety of plum. The gage was originally imported from Armenia and grows best in the south as it appreciates warmth.

Damsons are plentiful in countryside hedgerows, but if you live in a town or a city you may wish to grow your own. They have an advantage over plums and gages in that they are very hardy and much more tolerant of cold and wet situations. The black fruit is too sharp to be eaten without cooking, but it is glorious in puddings – damson and apple crumble is sublime – and makes delicious, strongly flavoured preserves.

PEAR *(Pyrus communis)*

Only a few varieties of pear ever make it on to the supermarket shelves, but there are many hundreds of varieties that the enthusiast can grow. They appreciate a sheltered, sunny spot and, because they flower earlier in the season than apples, their blossom is even more vulnerable to frost damage. Planting should ideally be undertaken in November, but can take place until March and the trees appreciate a mulch of manure every January or February. Fruiting will suffer in times of drought if the plant is not well watered. Pears are not self-fertile, so two or more plants will be required and these need to be close by to ensure cross-fertilisation. When buying, be sure to get compatible varieties. Half standards should be planted within 6m (20ft) of each other, cordons within 90cm (3ft) and espaliers within 4.5m (15ft). Most pears fruit on spurs and the branches need to be shortened to promote fruiting. Keep the centre of the tree open by annual pruning in winter. The fruit does not need to be thinned as extensively as apples, but it is sensible to reduce quantities to just one or two fruit per cluster. Pears are ripe when the fruit easily separates from the tree with a gentle twist, as with apples.

SOFT FRUIT: CURRANTS AND BERRIES – AND EVERYTHING ELSE

There is an argument to accepting that soft fruit is irresistibly attractive to birds and should only be grown in a fruit cage. This is a head-height, walk-in construction of wooden uprights with a ceiling and walls of fine-gauge net (see colour section for illustration). The roof should be removed every winter to let the birds get at the pests and to avoid the netting caving in under the weight of wet leaves or snow. Alternatively, you can just net individual bushes later in the season, though this is not so effective.

BLUEBERRY (*Vaccinium corymbosum*)

These North-American natives are massively popular fruit and can be grown without much fuss as long as your soil is acid (with a pH of 4.5–5.5) and is moisture retentive. Don't rule them out if you love them but your soil is too alkaline: they can be grown in containers or raised beds but it will be a lot of work. They do need plenty of water, so fare better in damp and waterlogged areas and often do best near a pond; a good thick mulch will help with moisture retention. Fruit is borne on the most vigorous shoots produced the previous summer. The plant needs little pruning in its first three years: after that the aim is, as ever, to produce an open bush and to cut out old or crossing shoots. Cut some branches to the base to encourage new growth and prune away around 15 per cent of the old growth.

CURRANTS (*Ribes* sp.)

Blackcurrants (*Ribes nigrum*) have the double benefit of being incredibly easy to grow and fantastically good for you – they are gloriously rich in vitamin C. The fruit is mouth-puckeringly tart raw, but is blissful in pies, crumbles, jams and ice creams. The bushes need a good, rich, moisture-retentive soil to crop really well, but they are most obliging plants and will tolerate neglect and shade and still produce fruit. The fruit grows on new wood, so after planting cut shoots back to two buds from the base to encourage new growth. If you have the space, plant a mix of varieties to ensure a continual crop from June to October and space them at 1.5m (5ft) intervals. Every autumn cut out the wood that has fruited, leaving only the new shoots – reducing the bush by one third to a half in the process.

Redcurrants (*Ribes rubrum*) and whitecurrants (a cultivar of *R. rubrum*), while close relatives of the blackcurrant, do not have quite the same requirements – they do not demand such rich soil and will tolerate shady conditions. They also differ by flowering on old wood: the pruning method dictates that branches are reduced in size, by about half, to an outward-facing bud, late each winter. The centre of the bush should be kept open and airy so that it is shaped like a wine glass. Fruit is produced in summer and will last well until the autumn on the bush. Redcurrants and whitecurrants are both high in pectin so are often mixed with other fruit in jam making. Mature bushes can produce more than 5kg (11lb) of fruit a year – fortunately it freezes easily!

JEAN'S SUMMER PUDDING

A good summer pudding is out of this world and I tried for years to make a good one – finally I asked my best friend's mother for her recipe, which tastes delicious and works like a charm.

225g (8oz) redcurrants
110g (4oz) blackcurrants
450g (1lb) raspberries
150g (5oz) caster sugar
Approximately 8 slices of white bread (with crusts removed)

Rinse the berries and cook in a large saucepan with the sugar for up to five minutes maximum. Lightly grease a 1½ pint pudding basin with butter and then line it with the bread. Overlap the slices and press well to seal. Fill in any gaps to prevent the juice from escaping. Pour in all the fruit but reserve a cupful of juice. Cover the pudding with another slice of bread then with a small saucer or plate, which fits into the top of the basin, and place a 1.5kg (3lb) weight on top of that. Leave in the fridge overnight. Just before serving, turn the pudding basin out on to a plate and spoon the reserved juice over any remaining bits of white bread. Serve with double cream or ice cream.

GOOSEBERRY *(Ribes uva-crispa)*

The gooseberry is a most underrated fruit with an ill-deserved reputation for sharp acidity. The fruit is tart, but it should also be juicy and sweet and the home-grown gooseberry is vastly superior in taste and quality to the overly firm, thick-skinned fruit sold in shops. Berries comes in a range of colours, with yellow and red flesh as well as the more familiar green; each has its own distinctive flavour. Some varieties are ideal for cooking, but others are perfect eaten raw. They will grow in sun or semi shade, but will not tolerate late frosts.

Ideally plant bushes in October for the best start, but they can be planted out until March. Dig in plenty of manure and space at a distance of 1.5m (5ft). A top-dressing of manure every spring will be appreciated. The bushes are best pruned to create a goblet shape, keeping the centre nice and airy, and taking out crossing and inward-growing branches. Caterpillars can be a problem – pick them off and remove them from the area. Thin fruit when it appears so that there is a distance of around 7.5mm (⅓in) between fruit. Bushes will fruit from May to August; the berries freeze well and make delicious desserts, jams and purées. A bush can be productive for 20 years and can produce 4–5kg (9–11lb) of fruit a year.

RASPBERRY *(Rubus idaeus)*

The raspberry is a perfect fruit to grow: not only is the fruit superb – equally good raw or cooked, on its own or teamed with other fruit – but it is also deliciously easy to grow. Ten canes will produce around 5kg (11lb) of fruit per year for around twelve years. As well as the traditional red fruit, yellow, gold, black and purple varieties are also available, though these are a little more delicate than their sturdier relative and they can fruit in early summer or autumn. Raspberries enjoy cool, damp conditions, which is why they fare so well in Scotland. They are best planted in November or December in an area that recieves partial sunshine. Although they like plenty of water they do not like having wet feet and good, deep, rich soil is required. Dig some manure into the soil a month before planting and feed with fertiliser or a mulch of compost every spring. Canes should be planted at a distance of around 50cm (20in) and rows spaced 1.8m (6ft) apart. Pruning is important for the production of bumper crops and summer- and autumn-fruiting varieties need different treatments. Summer-fruiting varieties fruit on one-year-old canes and are best grown on a post-and-wire system which supports the young canes through winter and ensures good air circulation, which helps prevent mildew and rotting (see colour section for illustration). Cut down the fruiting canes, but retain six to eight young canes that have yet to bear fruit. Tie these on to wire supports and in spring prune them to a healthy bud at the top to ensure they do grow above the height of the wires. Autumn-fruiting raspberries are sturdier and do not need post-and-wire support unless your situation is very windy. Canes should be cut down to the ground in late winter; the fruit will be produced on the new canes the following autumn.

JILL'S RASPBERRY SOUFFLÉ

275g (9oz) raspberries
3 or 4 egg whites
75g (3oz) caster sugar
Icing sugar for sifting

Grease a 15cm (6in), 6cm (2½in) deep soufflé dish with butter, then coat evenly with caster sugar (put a few teaspoons of sugar into the dish and swish it around until it sticks to the butter, giving it a frosty coating; tip out any excess sugar). Push the raspberries through a nylon sieve to make a seed-free purée – you need about 225g (8oz) of it. Whisk the egg whites thoroughly until stiff, but not dry, then gradually whisk in the caster sugar, whisking until shiny. Lightly fold (don't beat or over mix) the raspberry purée into the egg whites. Pour the soufflé mixture into the prepared dish, finishing with a swirl on top. Stand the dish on a baking tray and bake at 180°C (350°F or gas mark 4) for 20 minutes until set and starting to colour lightly on top. Remove from the oven and sift a little icing sugar on top – take to the table as is and serve immediately. Delicious!

RHUBARB *(Rheum x hybridum)*

There shouldn't be an allotment in the land that doesn't have a rhubarb plant growing on it somewhere. One or two of these no-nonsense plants will produce enough red stalks to feed the family for months, especially if you force some early stems in January. To harvest, pull stems by twisting them rather than cutting with scissors. Rhubarb will grow almost anywhere, in sun or shade, but it prefers a sunny spot. It isn't bothered by many pests or diseases. Exercise a little restraint in the first few years and you will get a really strong and vigorous plant; don't eat any stems in the first year and pick sparingly for a couple of years, as with asparagus (see page 37). Dig over the area where the rhubarb is to be planted in advance and incorporate plenty of manure. Plant out in March or October and feed with a mulch of manure every spring.

To force the plant, lift the crown and turn it over to expose the roots to frost – which pushes it into dormancy early in the season. Lift it into a box or pot and put it in a dark shed – you may need to cover it with bin bags to ensure that it really is in the dark. Rhubarb can be forced in the garden by covering the crown in early February with a large box or bucket. Plants that have been lifted for forcing can be replanted, but take a little while to recover. Do be aware that while the stalks are delicious, the leaves are very toxic.

STRAWBERRY (Fragaria x ananassa)

Picked and eaten fresh, strawberries are unsurpassable. If you want a crop the following year they should be planted in late summer – in good rich soil that has had plenty of farmyard manure dug in. If planted in the spring all flowers should be cut off over the summer for better fruiting the following year. Plants should be discarded after three years of fruiting, though they will throw out runners which you can pot up and use to increase your stock (see below and colour section for illustration). To ensure a constant supply, replace a third of your plants every year. Space plants at 45cm (18in) intervals in rows that are 75cm (30in) apart. Don't let weeds grow up between the rows and put down straw around the plants to keep the fruit away from the soil. Water in dry weather, but take care not to water the plant directly as this will damage the fruit. Remove any spoiled or rotting fruit and remove and compost the straw when fruiting is over.

FLOWERS

*Growing flowers on the allotment may not seem as
environmentally sound as growing your own food, but many
of the arguments for raising your own fruit and veg can
equally be applied to cut flowers for the house. Cut flowers
can travel just as many air miles as green beans and they
cost a small fortune. Organic gardeners appreciate the
benefits of specific companion plants and all flowers will
attract pollinating insects and birds.*

Home-grown cut flowers have a charm all of their own – it's
why we fall with such delight on the bunches of cut flowers
in a bucket at the end of someone's drive, with a tin for the
money. Their hotchpotch of colour and bloom has a *joie de
vivre* that flowers bought from the florist, beautiful and stylish
though they are, simply never achieve. Moreover some flowers
perform better in an allotment environment. They enjoy the
open aspect and thrive in tidy, structured, supported rows.
Their beauty is in their individual bloom and not in the
growing plant. When flowering is complete, they can be dug
up and the void they leave does not impact as it does in the
garden at home. Annuals such as snapdragons (*Antirrhinum*)
and cornflowers (*Centaurea cyanus*) can be sown in batches for
successive flowering, much as you would a salad crop, so that
the supply is constant. Brightly coloured nasturtiums
(*Tropaeolum majus*) make a valuable companion crop.

CHRYSANTHEMUM (*Chrysanthemum*)

Chrysanthemums have become a by-word for the ultimate
in bad taste, a reputation hastened by ghastly forecourt

bouquets. Fashion being what it is, chrysanthemums are ripe
for a return to favour. They are exceptional flowers: hardy,
easy to grow and prolific bloomers from August to November,
when everything else is dying down. Key to success is in
selecting hardy varieties – which can be challenging, since
enthusiasts have bred an exotic and extensive range of
delicate cultivars that require considerable pampering. Hardy
chrysanthemum cultivars come in a range of shapes and sizes
from the tall to the small. Korean varieties, which originate
from plants bred in America from seed collected in Korea by
EH Wilson in the 1920s, are taller. Rubellums are smaller
and were bred in the UK in the 1930s. Plants can last for
three to four years, after which time they become woody
and unproductive. At this point they should be lifted, the
old wood cut away and the fresh growth replanted.

Chrysanthemums enjoy an open sunny spot that does not
become waterlogged in winter – too much moisture around
the roots will kill the plant. They are greedy plants and need
plenty of compost or well-rotted manure dug in before
planting; a mulch of manure around the plants every spring
will also be appreciated. Favourites include a deep red variety
called 'Agnes Ann'; 'Ruby Mound', a tough plant that doesn't
need staking; and 'Topsy' with gold and rust flowers.

DAHLIAS (Dahlia)

Christopher Lloyd, the late gardening writer and owner of the
sumptuous gardens at Great Dixter in Kent, championed the
much-maligned dahlia for many years. Like chrysanthemums
the dahlia had acquired a tacky, overblown and garish image.
Lloyd appreciated the charm of the flower and valued its
intense jewel-like colours and distinctive, often architectural

appearance. Dahlias are statement flowers, and they make magnificent cut flowers for the home. There are more than 5,000 varieties, so there is quite a selection, with flowers that come in pompom, water lily or cactus shapes, from just 4cm (2in) across to monsters with flower faces of 30cm (1ft) – and all in a breathtaking palette of colours.

Plant tubers in late March or April in an open, sunny situation, when the soil has begun to warm up. Set them in plenty of compost in trenches around 15cm (6in) deep, with the eye facing upwards, at a distance of 45–60cm (18–24in). Slugs are passionate about dahlias and it really is worth ringing plants with grit to try to keep the slimy beasts at bay. Pinch out the growing stem to encourage plants to bush out and produce more flowers. Stake them early in the season – this is often best done at planting – as they are susceptible to wind damage. For exhibition, remove the two side buds so that all the plant's energy goes into the main flower.

Lift the plants when the first frost arrives, cutting stems back to within 5cm (2in) of the ground. Hang them upside down for a few days to dry them out and then store in dry compost in darkness until spring (see colour section for illustration). In theory you should check the tubers weekly, but who has the time?

POT MARIGOLD *(Calendula officinalis)*

The pot marigold, a hardy annual, is one of the easiest flowers to grow and it will go on flowering virtually throughout the year in the south. This sunny orange flower does have some culinary use: the petals have a mild, warm and fragrant flavour; they can also be used as a pale food dye and to replace saffron in recipes. The pot marigold's principal use in the allotment is as a companion plant to lure desirable predators into the vicinity to snack on your pests. Do not confuse them with French, African or Mexican marigolds (*Tagetes*), which are also used as companion plants but do not have edible petals.

SUNFLOWERS *(Helianthus annuus)*

Sunflowers are the most satisfying, trouble-free annuals, easy to sow straight into the ground when all danger of frosts has passed. These yellow giants, which can reach 3m (10ft) in height, have a charm and beauty all of their own – no matter how old and jaded you are. The individual florets, which mature into bird-friendly sunflower seeds, grow in a mathematically precise pattern of interconnecting spirals, typically 34 in one direction and 55 in the other. The head of the flower will follow the sun from east to west over the course of the day. Thin seedlings so that the plants are around 30–60cm (1–2ft) apart.

SWEET PEAS *(Lathyrus odoratus)*

Sweet peas are easy to grow and produce masses of fragrant flowers – the more you pick, the more you get. The best sweet peas are sown in the autumn (soak dark-coloured seeds overnight in water before planting) and overwintered in a cold frame, before being planted out in the spring. The plants need a framework of tall canes for support: plant one seedling at the base of each cane. The secret to producing glorious blooms is to pinch out side shoots and tendrils to concentrate the plant's energy into producing good stem growth and large flowers on long stalks.

NATURE'S EXCESS

*Nothing can beat the thrill when you spy your first runner
bean, courgette, pea pod or raspberry, or dig up the earliest
potatoes or carrots. The downside comes when you have
passed the first flush of enthusiasm and you are weighed
down by the fruitful abundance of your plot. It may feel like
you are producing three-quarters of a ton of food a month,
not a year. Bulging bags of produce are dragged home to a
family that becomes sick of the glut. 'Not beans again!' they
cry in unison.*

Betty MacDonald struggled to cope with over-production in
her autobiographical tale *The Egg and I*:

*'I crouched beneath the weight of an insupportable burden
every time I went out into the garden. Never have I come
face to face with such productivity. Pea vines pregnant
with bulging pods; bean poles staggering under big beans,
middle-sized beans, little beans and more blossoms; carrots
with bare shoulders thrust above the ground to show me
they were ready; succulent summer squash and zucchini
where it seemed only a matter of hours ago there were
blossoms; and I picked a water bucket full of cherries
from one lower branch of the old-fashioned late cherry
tree that shaded the kitchen. There was more of everything
than we could ever use or preserve and no way to absorb
the excess.'*

The main solution is, of course, to work out precisely what
you require – and grow accordingly, with just a little excess
allowance. Let's be realistic here: one family will never eat

300 lettuces a month – no matter how crisp and delicious they are. It just ain't humanly possible. So plan your crops carefully and thin your seedlings ruthlessly: a productive allotment has no room for sentiment.

HARVESTING

It is not always easy to tell when food is ready to be eaten. The simplest way is to keep tasting it – don't ever risk leaving things too late. Fruit and veg will taste their very best when they are perfectly mature – neither under nor over ripe. If you organise your time and you know you have a large crop waiting for you, the best time to pick most food is early in the morning, or late in the day when temperatures are lower. This is particularly so for leafy vegetables such as spinach, sprouting broccoli and lettuces, which will wilt in the heat. Some root crops will sit happily in the soil until required, but should only be dug up when the soil is dry. Carrots, turnips and swedes can be stored in darkness in boxes of sand in a cool, dry, frost-free environment. Potatoes also need darkness – think of how they are stored in the greengrocers in hessian or paper sacks and you have the idea. Many allotment holders become expert at persuading grocers to let them recycle these containers. One rule holds true for all vegetables – eat anything that looks less than perfect first – it won't store well no matter what it is.

Beans and peas need to be cropped continuously throughout the growing season – if they are left they become tough and unpalatable. Pick them and freeze them in small batches that you can use throughout the winter. Most onions should be dug up and left in the sunshine for a few days. They can be

89

strung up to hang in long strings or plaits in a dry environment. Squashes need to sit in the sun for a few weeks after harvesting for their flavour to mature, before being stored somewhere cool. Specific storage advice is given under fruit and vegetable listings where relevant.

PRESERVING FRUIT AND VEG

It is all too easy to freeze everything you have a glut of – but this is the time to be creative in your approach. If you have too many tomatoes, make chutney and all manner of pasta sauces. Make jam, jellies, pickles – sweet and savoury – conserves, sauces, ketchups, relish, syrups, cordials and ice cream. Get your recipe books out and stretch yourself. Effort expended now will mean you can wear the halo of a true domestic goddess – or god –throughout the winter. There is a world of difference between a shop-bought pasta sauce and one you made months earlier from your own allotment produce. This can extend into all kinds of frozen dishes: let's face it, if you can buy it as a frozen ready meal, you can also freeze it yourself.

If all else fails, sling a mass of vegetables into a pan and make great vats of soup for freezing. Save glass jars and bottles throughout the year for your preserving frenzy and save plastic containers for freezing. If possible, plan what you want to cook well in advance and set aside whole days to tackle food mountains in a creative way – you will feel tired, but impossibly smug when you have finished.

Always remember before you start that freezing is not a permanent solution to food storage – everything has a shelf life and most fruit and vegetables should be eaten within six months. Label and date everything! Only freeze top-quality fruit and vegetables: never include anything that is over-ripe or damaged.

Fruit should be frozen as soon as possible after picking. The trick is to freeze individual fruits spaced out on trays and then bag them up together when frozen; use a straw to suck air out of the bag before sealing it. This method is particularly suitable for berry fruit. Fruit can also be tossed in sugar before freezing: the sugar absorbs the fruit juice and a glorious sweet syrup is produced on defrosting. This works well with berry fruit that is going to be used in cooked desserts or to make jam or ice cream.

Apples and plums can be cooked before freezing – hard work now but blissful when your dessert is plucked from the freezer ready cooked. If you don't have time to make jam there and then, you can stew fruit without sugar, mash it and freeze it – then defrost it when you do have some spare time.

The secret to freezing vegetables is to prepare them as usual for cooking, then blanch them for just a couple of minutes in boiling, salted water – this halts enzyme activity which would otherwise affect flavour, nutritional value and colour. After blanching, run the veg under cold water, spread out to dry and then freeze.

The best vegetables of all are cooked fresh and in season. Wash them thoroughly to remove any soil residue, which will impair flavour. Don't take off too much flesh when removing the skin – keep peelings thin as most of the nutrition is just underneath the surface.

Steaming is the healthiest way to cook vegetables; it preserves nutrients as well as texture and flavour. If you have an allotment you really should treat yourself to a steamer to maximise health and taste benefits. As a general rule, steaming takes twice as long as boiling, and the process works best if vegetables are chopped so that they are all roughly the same size. Steamers with several layers enable you to steam two or three vegetables at the same time.

Green vegetables should be cooked in water that is already boiling; root vegetables should be started off in cold water. Cooking times vary according to taste, but the golden rule with leafy vegetables is to remove them from the cooking process when they are slightly underdone as they continue to cook for a short time afterwards – this ensures that they are perfect, not spoiled, when they are served up.

Stir fries are delicious: the secret is to use hot oil, to chop vegetables very small, never to cook too many at once and stir constantly. Start with the vegetables that take longer to cook and add the ones that just need a moment at the last minute.

USEFUL ORGANISATIONS

**AUDLEY END ORGANIC
KITCHEN GARDEN**
Saffron Walden,
Essex CB11 4JG
*A beautifully restored kitchen garden,
as it would have been at the end of
the 19th century. Part of the Yalding
Organic Gardens (see page 94) in
association with English Heritage.*

**BROGDALE HORTICULTURAL
TRUST**
Brogdale Farm, Brogdale Road,
Faversham, Kent ME13 8XZ
www.brogdale.org
*Home of the National Fruit
Collection.*

**DEPARTMENT FOR
ENVIRONMENT, FOOD AND
RURAL AFFAIRS (DEFRA)**
Nobel House, 17 Smith Square,
London SW1P 3JR
www.defra.gov.uk
*DEFRA is a UK government
department managing issues such as
the environment, rural development,
the countryside, wildlife and
sustainable development.*

**NATIONAL SOCIETY OF
ALLOTMENT & LEISURE
GARDENERS**
O'Dell House, Hunters Road,
Corby, Northants NN17 5JE
www.nsalg.org.uk
*A united voice for the Allotment
Movement, aiming to preserve, protect
and promote a traditional way of life.*

FRESH FOOD CENTRAL
www.freshfoodcentral.com
*Information about seasonal fruit
and vegetables.*

**THE NATIONAL ALLOTMENT
GARDENERS TRUST**
PO Box 1448, Marston,
Oxford OX3 3AY
www.nagtrust.org
*A charity promoting the benefits of
allotment holding and recreational
gardening.*

NATIONAL VEGETABLE SOCIETY
5 Whitelow Road, Heaton Moor,
Stockport SK4 4BY
www.nvsuk.org.uk
*The NVS is a charity dedicated to
advancing the culture, study and
improvement of vegetables and
offering help and advice to novices.*

**ROYAL HORTICULTURAL
SOCIETY**
80 Vincent Square,
London SW1P 2PE
www.rhs.org.uk
*The UK's leading gardening charity,
dedicated to advancing horticulture
and promoting good gardening.*

RHS GARDEN WISLEY
Woking,
Surrey GU23 6QB
www.rhs.org.uk
*Glorious RHS gardens and a great
fruit and vegetable garden.*

**SCOTTISH ALLOTMENTS AND
GARDENS SOCIETY**
www.sags.org.uk
*SAGS works for allotment sites and
plot holders throughout Scotland.*

SOIL ASSOCIATION
South Plaza, Marlborough Street,
Bristol BS1 3NX
www.soilassociation.org
*The UK's leading environmental
charity promoting sustainable organic
farming and championing human and
environmental health.*

SELF SUFFICENT 'ISH'
www.selfsufficientish.com
*Advice and information on anything
self-sufficientish.*

YALDING ORGANIC GARDENS
Benover Road, Yalding,
Nr. Maidstone, Kent ME18 6EX.
www.marofoods.co.uk/ and click
on Yalding
*Formerly part of Garden Organic but
now under new ownership. Yalding
has a beautiful fruit garden.*

BIBLIOGRAPHY

Complete Guide to Home Gardens
(Associated Newspapers Ltd)

Food from Your Garden & Allotment
(Reader's Digest, 2008)

Food from Your Garden (Reader's
Digest, 1977)

Grow Your Own Veg, Carol Klein
(Mitchell Beazley, 2007)

Kitchen Garden, Lucy Peel (Collins,
2003)

Bob Flowerdew's Organic Bible (Kyle
Cathie, 1998)

Pippa's Organic Kitchen Garden,
Pippa Greenwood (Dorling
Kindersley, 1999)

The Allotment Book, Andi Celevely
(Collins, 2006)

*Practical Gardening and Food
Production,* Richard Sudell
(Odhams Press Limited)

The Allotment Gardener's Cookbook
(Reader's Digest, 2007)

The Allotment Handbook, Caroline
Foley (New Holland Publishers
(UK) Ltd, 2004)

The Complete Gardener, W.E.
Shewell-Cooper (Collins, 1950)

The Egg and I, Betty MacDonald
(George Mann
of Maidstone, 1992; first published
1945)

The Prickotty Bush, Monty Don
(Macmillan London
Ltd, 1990)

AUTHOR'S ACKNOWLEDGEMENTS

I am grateful to Ann and Peter Sutherland who generously wasted hours of their time talking allotments with me and showering me with produce and recipes. Similarly Geoff Stokes, National Secretary of the NSALG was a goldmine of useful information and my best friend Jill Alkin and her mother, Jean Alkin, have kindly kept me supplied with wonderful recipes over the years. Thanks also to my family, Eric, Lou, Florence, Teddy and Genevieve, who are, as always, tolerant of my various obsessions. They gamely try every new vegetable I throw at them, though my eldest, Florence, occasionally baulks on the grounds that some look 'suspicious'. I must also thank the allotment holders at Ash, Kent, who were very tolerant of my first attempts at growing fruit and veg. They were positively indulgent towards my, then, small children and without that kindness I could not have managed. Finally thanks to Tina Persaud, Polly Powell, and Kristy Richardson at Anova, who are preternaturally kind, patient and encouraging.

INDEX